UNDERSTANDING ASSESSMENT

IN DESIGN AND TECHNOLOGY

MANAGING AUTHORS
Ali Farrell
Jim Patterson

CONTRIBUTING AUTHORS
Jo Compton
Paddy O'Hagan

for the
TECHNOLOGY EDUCATION
RESEARCH UNIT
GOLDSMITHS' COLLEGE
UNIVERSITY OF LONDON

Hodder & Stoughton
LONDON SYDNEY AUCKLAND

Acknowledgements

TERU wishes to acknowledge the following schools who gave permission for their pupils' work to be included in this book. Actual pupil names have been changed.

Collingwood, Surrey
Copland Community School, Brent
Copthall, Barnet
Dwr–y–Felin, West Glamorgan
Grays School, Essex
Joseph Eastham School, Salford
Heath End School, Surrey
West Hatch, Essex
Ladymead, Somerset
Mark Rutherford, Bedfordshire
Parkview, Cumbria
Riddlesdown, Croydon
Rodborough, Surrey
Queen Elizabeth Grammar, Wakefield
Wells Blue School, Somerset

British Library Cataloguing in Publication Data

Technology Education Research Unit
  Understanding Assessment in Design and Technology
  I. Title
  745.4

ISBN 0 340 57305 8

First published 1993

Impression number   10 9 8 7 6 5 4 3 2 1
Year   1998 1997 1996 1995 1994 1993

© 1993 TERU, Goldsmiths' College, University of London

Typeset by Multiplex Techniques Limited
Printed in Hong Kong for the educational publishing division of Hodder & Stoughton Ltd, Mill Road, Dunton Green, Sevenoaks, Kent by Colorcraft Ltd

Contents

1 Introduction 1

2 Understanding capability 3

3 Assessment issues 7

4 Assessing capability: 24
   Working with graphic materials 26
   Working with food materials 44
   Working with resistant materials 68
   Working with textiles 98

5 Planning assessments 122

**Understanding Assessment in
Design and Technology**

Planning to Assess Learning

	What are you intending that pupils should learn?	How will you achieve this?	What do you want to assess through this activity?	How will you get pupils to generate that evidence?
What is your activity/ starting point/theme/ topic?	• concepts of . . . • knowledge about . . .	*examples: skills sessions, taught input, demonstrations, use of audio-visual aids, use of printed resources, short focussed activities, scientific investigations etc.*	**Is its purpose:** ☐ formative? ☐ diagnostic? ☐ summative?	*examples: through worksheets, discussion, their use of tools, materials and processes, their integration of knowledge and understanding, oral questionning, presentation, working notes and drawings, test questions etc.*
What year group are you planning for?	• understanding of . . . • skills/techniques in . . .		**And is it:** ☐ at profile component (PC) level only, to produce an assessment of overall capability? ☐ each of the ATs to produce a detailed assessment?	
What materials base will pupils work in?	• issues re . . . • processes of . . . • other . . .		☐ each of the ATs plus an overall PC level? ☐ selected skills, qualities, knowledge, understanding that you want to check against criteria other than the SoA in the Order?	

1 Introduction

Assessment, within the National Curriculum as elsewhere, should directly relate to pupils' learning and progression. The intentions behind appraising pupils' performances are:

- determining whether pupils are learning and progressing as expected
- identifying a pupil's strengths and weaknesses, so that positive achievement can be recognized and learning difficulties supported
- seeing how well the teaching programme has achieved its aims.

Design and technology (d&t) capability is assessed using a variety of evidence (including outcomes, documentation, graphics and photographs) supplemented by the teacher's perception and knowledge of how pupils do things.
For example, how they:

- interact with materials, tools and processes
- grapple with ideas and issues
- reflect whilst also being active
- interact and collaborate with others
- express themselves
- pursue and develop ideas
- reason, justify and are critical about the what, how and why of their d&t activity.

This book aims to set d&t assessment into a manageable framework. It puts the complex and related issues of the National Curriculum into perspective, so clarifying them and it suggests practical ways of confronting these issues.

Its purpose is to help you to come to terms with a range of curriculum and assessment matters of prime importance. These include how to:

- ensure that d&t activities provide

opportunities to assess a pupil's capability
- manage such activities to ensure that opportunities are fully realized
- ensure learning and progression during project work
- recognize evidence of d&t capability
- help pupils communicate their ideas
- encourage pupils to generate evidence for assessment
- decide what to base assessments on
- use teacher intervention as part of assessment
- involve pupils in evaluating themselves and their work as part of d&t capability
- consider how much evidence and assessment information needs to be recorded
- interpret pupils' attainments against National Curriculum statements
- attribute National Curriculum levels to a pupil's work
- make assessments consistent across a range of specialist teachers.

USING THIS BOOK

Chapters two and three look at some of the assessment issues which are of concern to d&t teachers. The text is cross-referenced to examples of project work which illustrate the issues under discussion.

Chapter four presents a further selection of pupils' work in a variety of media and across a range of National Curriculum levels. Each is accompanied by a commentary on the strengths and weaknesses of the capability being demonstrated, so helping you to form your own opinions and judgements in relation to the model evidence and assessment.

By engaging in the suggested activities, you can consider for yourself how issues similar to those raised by these projects might be tackled and resolved in your own classroom. These exercises can be carried out by teachers individually, or as the basis of in-service sessions, ideally with a group or department of teachers working together. They provide a focused resource for teachers' developing understanding and expertise in the concepts and practice of National Curriculum assessment.

We have chosen to demonstrate capability through extended d&t projects. It is worth pointing out, however, that just because teachers are aiming to develop pupils' holistic capability, this does not mean that all activities themselves have to be holistic. There are many activities and experiences of different types, lengths and styles which can contribute towards pupils becoming capable. Particular aspects of capability might well be taught and acquired through a variety of more focused activities during a key stage learning programme.

Extended d&t projects are, however, particularly useful in providing pupils with the opportunity to interact (holistically) within and across the processes of all Attainment Targets, and draw on the knowledge, skills and understanding (from the Programme of Study). They challenge pupils to show their full capability rather than single aspects of it. For this reason extended projects, through which whole capablility can be assessed, have been chosen as the focus of this book.

2 *Understanding Capability*

Capability involves being able to combine practical action with deepening understanding. It is a measure of your 'power' in taking action and clarifying understanding, i.e. how in tune and developed your actions and understanding are. Capability is based on the need to intervene, clarify what we see in our mind's eye, make value judgements and put them to the test of reality. It thrives on the need for purposeful acquisition of knowledge and skills. It depends on being able to step back to take an overview as well as to focus on details within an activity.

Capability is more than a collection of separate abilities. For example, you may be able to ride a bike but are you a capable cyclist? Would you let a child embark on a solo ride across a strange city in the middle of winter? Could you learn capability as a theory and be confident that in the real world you could make it happen? Could you simply practise skills in your street and be sure of being capable elsewhere?

We should not be surprised when pupils who are taught particular abilities without a view of capability, find it hard to transfer them into new situations. Abilities are often disconnected from the reality of life. How long would you survive on a bike if you could only balance, steer, brake and pedal? Capability gives you the means to operate in and be part of the changing and developing world. It helps the individual to develop a clearer overview of what is involved and how they might move forward. This is the essence of learning.

Developing capability is a slow process. It relies on teachers providing purposeful experiences matched to capability, where action can be taken, new knowledge gained, skills tried and practised, and understanding developed. For example, once a person is a really capable cyclist in all situations, then it is a small step to imagine him or her becoming a capable motorist or traffic controller.

WHAT IS DESIGN AND TECHNOLOGY?

Design and technology offers many opportunities for people to develop their capability. In particular, to intervene for themselves in the 'made' world by designing and making products and systems to meet people's needs. As a result, they will better understand the pressures that operate in the real world of people, products, systems and our environment. The processes of *perception* (learning to see d&t), *generation* (learning to create and confront), and *critical thought* (learning to question and challenge) involved in developing d&t capability are central to our continuing education. The qualities(focuses and attitudes) implicit in d&t capability are central to our economic and social development as individuals and as a nation.

FOCUSES AND ATTITUDES

Design and technology involves identifying and responding to the real needs of people in their society; e.g. physical, emotional, economic, social and spiritual:

'If we could produce this faster we would have a competitive product'
'If we do that it will have a disastrous effect on the environment'
'It may be fine for you but we need a safer solution for the children'

'It's great because it lets me express my identity'
'It seems like a good idea but it would go against our cultural laws'
'We need to make sure growing toddlers have a nutritious diet'.

It is rich with opportunities to see how people's differing and changing needs and values are crucial for developing technology and vice versa:

'Fashion products at this price mean we can all afford them'
'I don't know how we managed before that was invented'
'I had to live near work to be able to get there on time'
'It used to take ages to get the message to everyone'
'This new material enables faster and cheaper production in meeting our needs'.

Design and technology illustrates clearly the importance we attach to forming and understanding our own values and respecting the values other people hold:

'We couldn't agree on the one we thought was best for everyone'
'Tom wouldn't be seen dead wearing one of those!'
'Some people will need this and won't be able to afford it'
'It will use less energy that way and that's a major consideration for me'.

It involves real products and systems that can be used, tested, evaluated, modified and which form the basis for new ideas:

'These are both about the same price but one is really difficult to use'
'If I changed the way it works it would be easier to make and still do the job'
'If I do it this way more people would use it'
'It is a quality product unlike the other one which is really tacky'.

It encourages people to learn to intervene practically by promoting the interdependence of thought and action:

'If I draw it this way it will help me to see the real problem'
'If I use another material it will be easier to make and stronger'
'If I try it out in 3D I will have a better idea of whether it works as I imagine'
'If it is made of x will people want to use it?'.

Design and technology encourages people to

be more autonomous learners who can operate independently and collaboratively as the occasion demands:

'I need to talk to Jane about my idea'
'If I brainstorm ideas with the team I might solve this problem'
'I need to find out for myself whether this will work'
'It's no good thinking that I know all the answers'.

ACTIVE AND REFLECTIVE LEARNERS

Using real world examples and developing the kinds of attitudes shown above requires children and students to be both *active* and *reflective*. This means not only confronting and clarifying what they are doing and how they are doing it, but also reconciling why they are doing it. However, if action dominates over reflection then skills maybe practised or knowledge gained but it will be unlikely that understandings will develop. Actions will have little connection with real world purpose and lose much of their long term educative value. Equally, if reflection dominates over action then it is likely that many issues will be considered but few of them will be confronted and clarified by action. Design and technology is based in the real world of products and people and *must* provide for children to develop practical strategies that confront the reality of their ideas and their understandings. For this to be both 'real' and purposeful it must be recognizable as part of their world and they must see the challenges as learning opportunities which they are motivated to pursue.

A helpful way of finding out whether or not pupils are working in this balanced way, is to look at examples of pupils' work and to consider where and how they are being active and reflective and where they are relating one to the other. Look at the three examples in chapter three. One is dominated by reflection (p.18) and one by actions (p.14). The third appears to have action and reflection working *iteratively* (p.22), that is, pupils to-ing and fro-ing between the need to confront reality and question validity which pushes progression in the outcome and progression in learning. The more capable pupils are, the more able they are to reflect whilst taking action and to act on their reflections.

Look at each example of work:

- Can you see where and how reflection has prompted action?
- Can you see when action has prompted more rigorous reflection?
- Are there places where there is little connection between reflection and action?
- What could you have done to help the unbalanced work become better balanced?
- Can you see where pupils were deficient in knowledge and understanding?
- Can you see where pupils were deficient in the skills to proceed?
- How would you have supported the development of sufficient knowledge and skill to support their progression in this activity?

Now that you have studied some projects which have been selected to highlight features of active and reflective learning, take a sample of work from your own pupils:

- do they reveal how children have taken action and reflected in order to proceed with more understanding?
- can you see progression in the outcome?
- can you see progression in pupils' learning?
- do the children identify their own progression? Are they aware of it?
- can you see that children have different starting points and develop ideas in different ways?

MAKING PROGRESS WITH CAPABILITY

Without sufficient knowledge and skill to sustain development, any understanding acquired can be trivial and result in superficial learning. Balancing carefully what pupils know, understand and can do, with their need to know and do more, is crucial to progression.

Close analysis of the Statements of Attainment (SoA) and Programmes of Study (PoS) across the ten National Curriculum levels helps to identify the features of progression in capability terms.

The following descriptions were devised using the National Curriculum to bring this progression into focus. They describe how pupils are operating with their knowledge, skill and understanding (in terms of capability) at particular levels.

LEVEL 3 DEVELOPING AWARENESS

Pupils will mainly be reporting on what has been done in simple terms and giving a picture of a series of separate actions. They should be giving simple reasons or making links between what they did and how or why it was like that.

LEVEL 4-5 MAKING SUITABLE CHOICES

The teacher will have been creating situations that enable pupils to take decisions but increasingly *to justify* why they made choices, worked or developed ideas in the way they did. Pupils should show their understanding through the *reasons* they give, in reflecting on their ideas and actions, and the connections between intent (it needs to be like this ...) and decision (so it will do that ...) and justification (because I know that...which makes it suitable for ...).

LEVEL 6-7 SPECULATING CRITICALLY ABOUT DECISIONS

Pupils' learning will have involved them in handling *a range* of variables, which are used in predicting *and* taking decisions to meet their identified *aims*. Pupils should show breadth and depth of understanding through the clarity with which they can articulate their *intentions and choices* in pursuing their *objectives*. They should be using their knowledge, skill and understanding to explain and justify the way they worked. There will be a clear impression of *connectedness* between aspects of their work (ideas to research; quality assurance in making to specification; testing to check on intentions satisfied).

Seen in this way, it becomes obvious that progression cannot be achieved by attending to individual Attainment Targets and Programmes of Study as if they were items to be addressed separately until 'enough' of them had been covered by pupils.

Progression in d&t terms is exemplified by looking at the Programmes of Study and the Statements of Attainment across any one level – as a bunch of characteristics which, taken together, describe capability by indicating what pupils should be capable of doing and with what knowledge, understanding and skill they are likely to be doing this.

3 Assessment Issues

Some of the issues discussed in this chapter are illustrated by the examples of projects which follow. Where this is the case the cross-reference is given in brackets. These projects have been chosen because they are particularly useful examples of the more problematic issues for evidence and assessment. They are not intended as a critique of individual pupil attainment, but are typical of the ways in which many pupils respond to d&t activities.

RECOGNIZING CAPABILITY

If we are trying to enable our pupils to become capable, it is important that we can recognize what this means in terms of what they do and how they do it. Assessment is a good means of monitoring how pupils are progressing and whether they are becoming more capable.

Until teachers become familiar with the Order for Technology, and its Attainment Targets and Statements of Attainment, it remains difficult to use them to make assessments. Perhaps the most obvious reason for this is the difficulty of using words that adequately express 'capability' to a range of teachers working with different subject and value backgrounds.

Another problem is that progression in capability cannot be represented in simple incremental steps. Like riding a bicycle you learn by concentrating on different aspects - pedalling or steering. Then quite suddenly you get the hang of it. You practise some more, in different circumstances or with different equipment, and gradually become more capable. Increasingly you can handle more variables and different challenges with broader and deeper understanding.

To help pupils become capable we try to

enable them to operate simultaneously the range of processes represented within the ATs, rather than exclusively developing one aspect at a time in a linear way. True capability will not develop where pupils are unaware of how the aspects of capability interact with, and inform one another.

ACTIVE AND REFLECTIVE BALANCE

The Statements of Attainment use both active and reflective terms to describe capability for assessment purposes and so it is important that you help pupils demonstrate and value these aspects of capability. They need to develop a vocabulary to express the what, how and why of their work. They will need help to record and communicate evidence of their thinking and actions during project work. This is so that others can see what they have been doing and why they arrived at a particular outcome as well as being purposeful to the development of their ideas. This recorded evidence can be very important for summative assessments when evidence has to be retained. You and your colleagues can use it as source material in discussions of the kinds of judgements you are making about the pupils' work, so that schools develop common standards.

Focusing on active and reflective capability and helping pupils to develop them interactively is important because:
1) Pupils who are allowed to concentrate on developing reflective ability, at the expense of active ability, typically will consider issues and make theoretical proposals. They will do so without confronting the technical and production issues of making their ideas work out in real terms. As a result, they produce much recorded evidence, in particular of appraising and researching, which appears to

generate evidence of some aspects of capability but little active development of ideas. (See Kay's work on p. 18.)

2) Pupils who are allowed to concentrate on developing active ability, at the expense of reflective ability, typically will 'do' things without reflecting on their actions or the issues surrounding their work. They are so intent on production that they do not pause long enough to appraise, show judgements, recognize the implications of decisions, review, modify or consider alternatives. They generate a disproportionate amount of evidence about what they do in relation to how their reflections are informing their actions. (See David's work on p. 14.)

From studying evidence exhibited and recorded during d&t activity, it is possible to monitor how far each pupil is working in a balanced way as opposed to mainly in the reflective *or* in the active aspect. Thus you can use formative assessment to diagnose pupils' strengths and weaknesses in these areas during the course of a project and summatively after the event. Then you can identify what needs to happen next for pupils to progress towards a more balanced capability.

In practice, this might mean that some pupils will need encouragement to confront their ideas through the manipulation of materials, tools and processes by building on the issues they have identified. If you encourage them to work from an area of strength they can be helped to progress with confidence towards a more balanced capability. They need to move away from safe and familiar ground and be supported whilst doing so. Kay would have benefited from this.

Those pupils (e.g. David) whose active ability predominates, need encouragement to reflect and confront the issues surrounding that activity, rather than being allowed to develop active ability at the expense of reflective qualities, e.g. pursuing a technical problem for its own sake and without any broader purpose in mind.

You can most clearly see fully developed capability in d&t when both reflective and active abilities are integrated in a pupil's response to a task. Consequently the pupil is working in a fairly balanced way, in terms of quality rather than quantity, across the ATs.

Whilst most pupils will exhibit areas of strength and weakness in attainment levels across the ATs, it is not wise to encourage wide discrepancies between AT scores, as this promotes pupils' strengths whilst maintaining their weaknesses. You have already seen the problems this causes in terms of how pupils work, in the above-mentioned projects.

To take the cycling analogy further, David is skilled in pedalling and steering, but his balance and braking are not in tune with this. Kay balances and brakes well, but doesn't move forward in terms of steering and pedalling. In neither case does this make for a capable cyclist!

KNOWLEDGE AND UNDERSTANDING

Whilst pupils are developing procedural capability (in investigating, generating, exploring, planning, specifying, making, evaluating) they should bring their knowledge and understanding of materials, people, technical and production matters and aesthetics to the task. Not just the possession of knowledge is required, but the appropriate or purposeful application of knowledge and understanding, of both conceptual and procedural matters, as an integral part of getting suitable ideas to happen. The facility to draw on and develop knowledge, skills and understanding from the Programmes of Study, whilst operating competently within and across the procedures of d&t, differentiates between pupils who are capable and those who are just 'doing' the design process or demonstrating skills and knowledge acquired in a discrete and disconnected way. (See Gareth's work on p.16.)

Once National Curriculum Programmes of Study have been fully established the evidence that pupils have been following them and can draw upon and demonstrate their knowledge and understanding within an activity should be apparent.

If pupils have not been taught the knowledge, skills and understanding set out in the Programme of Study at their level of capability, and if they do not have experience of appropriately drawing on it during d&t activity, they are unlikely to make progress from one level to another.

PUPILS' PERCEPTIONS

Pupils often perform for teachers in relation to what they think is being expected of them. So it is crucial that pupils have a clear view of what 'being capable' means. It is often very obvious, from the evidence generated by pupils in an activity, what they think the teacher is expecting. This particularly true of evaluating where there are three strands or aspects of evaluation to be assessed:
- a pupil's awareness of the design process and their use of resources
- his or her appraisal of outcomes against original intentions and
- his or her critical thoughts about the impact of d&t activity.

In looking at how the project is going and how they are working, pupils who think that effort, good presentation and finishing the project on time are the sole criteria against which they will be judged will think that they are capable if they have done these things well (e.g. Sue p.20).

Pupils who understand that capability is judged in relation to how well they manage and interact with the processes, concepts, materials and resources of d&t are more likely to produce evidence of capability because they have understood the purpose of what they are doing and are aware of what it is to be capable.

Capability can be explained to pupils by practical example where they are shown what constitutes capable ways of working. Once they are engaged in being capable within an activity you can use the evidence they generate for assessment and to give the pupils feedback on their achievements. This is a *curriculum-led* approach to assessment.

In the less desirable *assessment-driven* approach pupils are put into situations in order to display evidence of Statements of Attainment so that they may be assessed. This can confuse pupils because they are expected to jump through hoops and they are not sure what the hoops are or why they are jumping through them! The former approach depends on pupils understanding what it means to be capable and so helps them to know what is expected of them and what their attainments are.

RECORDING EVIDENCE

When you ask pupils to record their ideas, thinking and reasoning, they are actually being asked to communicate their ideas, explore and develop them:
1) as a means of confronting hazy ideas in a more concrete form to explore, develop and clarify them and
2) as a means of demonstrating why and in what ways they are being reflective and active. You can use this information in your assessments and it results in the recording of their dynamic progression instead of just what they have 'done' (coverage). So one focus of d&t teaching is enabling pupils to understand the purpose of records and developing their communication skills so they can make them.

This is distinctly different from pupils writing about what they are doing, where the focus of concern is in getting pupils to express and describe their thoughts and actions, recording coverage as an exercise in itself. Some evidence recorded in pupils' project work indicates recording for recording's sake, rather than what pupils are doing, thinking and trying to work out.

For example, drawing what something will look like can be a recording exercise, with the emphasis on producing (as in Carol's work on p. 12) the sketches, rather than this being a development exercise whereby pupils use drawings, sketches and graphic skills to show how they will get their ideas to move forward and work out. There is also a difference between pupils making a 3D representation of something they have represented in 2D, as opposed to modelling ideas in a concrete form using a range of materials and equipment, so being able to develop ideas by 'hands on' use of resources.

It is unlikely that the best way of developing ideas and recording evidence will be the same for all aspects of d&t. There are many things that go on during d&t activity that do not easily yield tangible evidence. Often pupils will be interacting with the teacher, with other pupils, or with materials and resources in ways which help them in the exploration and realization of ideas. Nevertheless, watching pupils engaged in this kind of activity can still inform the teacher's decisions about the pupil's capability and there is no necessity to record every aspect of evidence in a permanent form, especially if doing so serves no useful purpose.

COMMON ASSESSMENT PROBLEMS

QUALITY NOT QUANTITY

Pupils often talk about having done 'enough' research or 'enough' evaluation or of having had 'enough' ideas. This indicates that they believe quantity to be the measure the teacher will use in assessing their work. Teachers may share this misunderstanding if they perceive that d&t requires pupils to 'do' the Attainment Targets, as if each has a quantity of outcome which is judged, rather than representing the processes by which pupils achieve certain purposes.

Typically you can see pupils working, for instance on research, in an isolated way and not in the context of what they are setting out to achieve in their task. Similarly, they 'do' a piece of evaluation because the lesson begins with the teacher saying that today they will be doing evaluation, rather than because they are being encouraged to evaluate the what, how and why of their activity as an integral part of their working. Pupils who are allowed unthinkingly to work to short-term, outcome-dependent goals in this way tend to work in a linear fashion. Perhaps the answer to the question 'how much is *enough*?' is best deflected by another question 'how much/what is *appropriate*?'.

If pupils see the ATs as separate and unrelated to one another, and as something that they have to do to satisfy the teacher, then it will be difficult to assess their work using the Statements of Attainment (SoA) which describe capability. The SoA set out what pupils are expected to be able to do/achieve when assessed as being at a particular level. However, the SoA are not merely things which pupils need to demonstrate in order to be judged capable. Planning projects around the SoA as if they constituted a teaching model, as opposed to an assessment model, to guarantee the return of certain types of evidence, is likely to lead to pupils falsely showing evidence of a particular SoA. This is much less useful to the teacher or purposeful to the pupil, than pupils working in a capable manner and, in so doing, generating evidence of what they know, understand and can do. This can then be assessed against the SoA. Pupils therefore need to understand the assessment criteria, i.e. what it is they are being expected to do and demonstrate.

CAPABILITY NOT ABILITY

A pupil who is able is not necessarily capable. These two qualities are different (e.g. Gareth appears capable but is showing ability rather than capability in his well-wrought project).

Teachers sometimes mark a pupil's known ability, rather than his or her capability from the evidence of a d&t activity. A pupil may display a number or a range of separate abilities but be unable to interact with the processes of d&t at the same time as bringing breadth and depth of appropriate knowledge and understanding to bear on a task. Pupils may have put a considerable amount of time and effort into the work, or have done better than usual, but this does not necessarily indicate capability or progression in d&t terms. Sometimes it is difficult to separate what one knows and feels about a pupil when judging their achievements against objective performance criteria.

ASSESSING PROCESS

Where teachers are assessing work from pupils who have spent only a short amount of time being taught from the Programme of Study, their work is likely to show insufficient use of d&t concepts (knowledge and understanding) to aid progress within the processes of d&t (Attainment Target levels) and an over-reliance on common sense rather than design skills. Where d&t is new to pupils they may be working within their existing knowledge and understanding rather than being appropriately challenged to move forward (see Kay p.18).

In assessment it is important to look at the Programme of Study as well as the Statement of Attainment at any level, in order to identify the depth and breadth of knowledge and understanding with which pupils are operating and which they are bringing to bear on the process. As time goes by and each school gets a better view of what their pupils should be able to demonstrate then perhaps we will expect more evidence from our pupils of their knowledge and understanding about, e.g. graphic techniques, properties of materials, safe working practices, etc.

PUPIL RESPONSIBILITY FOR LEARNING

Many teachers initially interpreted National Curriculum d&t as a licence for pupils to do exactly as they want. This is unlikely to lead to a coherent curriculum with any certainty of progression, or of manageable assessment practice. With this approach pupils either get involved in unrealistic projects or work safely within their existing knowledge, skill and understanding, and are not stretched further. You need to set up structured activities and monitor your pupils' progress, intervening to check that what pupils are doing is achievable within the time and resources available. What is needed is appropriate teacher intervention based on diagnostic assessments, i.e. what stage have pupils reached in their work? What are they going to encounter/learn? How can I help them take the next step? It is worth considering, for each of the projects presented in this chapter, how you might have intervened in order to benefit pupils.

Assessment is not best approached with a 'hands-off' policy, whereby teachers sit back and observe what pupils can do when left without the teacher's support. Every intervention is an opportunity for assessment, as it involves you in making a judgement about the level and type of intervention which the pupil needs to proceed. This, in turn, says something about the level of autonomy and capability of the pupil. The responsibility which pupils take for their learning should match their level of capability and they will require teacher guidance for this, rather than the decision being handed over to them completely, (e.g. Vicky on p. 22).

CAROL

Carol's decisions about the artefact's design were made at an early stage rather than developed as a result of exploration and development through making. The motivating factor is the active pursuit of production with little reflection on how the product will be used or by whom, or why it is being produced.

This is, perhaps, a pupil who has not been expected (or taught how) to pursue ideas through their development, reconciling difficulties and conflicts along the way, but who is more used to making an idea they have had.

Carol is evidently able to come up with a purposeful and creative idea. Early prompting could have encouraged her to think about what she was doing and why, at all stages of her designing and making. What strategies could you use to encourage this way of working?

Agreed brief is:

To design a suitable measuring device to measure the temperature in a bedroom. It has to be able to hang on a wall. It will be made from wood & at a smallish size.

I think that the most important decisions that I wi big or small my end project will be & to try & to make my project work well I think I hard on what I am doing & try to make eve respectable.

decided to use wood because it has a nice texture & looks quite nice in a house. I decided to make it quite small because if it was big it would ake the thermometer look out of place. I have decided to make it or a bedroom because I think it would look nice hanging on a bedroom wall.

Hanger to put on wall
(behind sun)

wood

THERMOM

235

I chose this design because it was quite simple to make and it didn't have too much detail so it looked quite good as well.

o make are how as neat as possible ve to con'sentrate I do neat &

If I did my project again I would ~~make it~~ set it out better and give myself more time to make it better and I would make my ideas better.

DAVID

David is typical of those pupils who are predominantly active and reflect very little, even when actively engaged. He had an idea from a book and is intent on 'making it'.

He made a series of decisions about his chosen outcome which revolved around getting the windcatcher to work. It is difficult to claim that he explored, developed and refined ideas through working with materials, because his goal was to seek a solution rather than to model ideas.

You could say that David is working in context because his windcatcher relates to an element of the weather. However, it is more likely that he latched on to an idea that was suggested by the theme without fully engaging with the theme. This is common with pupils, and prompts us to question the usefulness and purpose of working with themes.

That is not to say that this was not a valid and worthwhile activity for David, who wanted to make something and followed this idea through to a made outcome with some success.

Yet it is a difficult piece of work from which to assess holistic capability because, whilst motivated by the activity, David is pursuing some interests and abilities whilst neglecting others and so is demonstrating these rather than capability.

The School made me decide on my brief be cause is to do with what we are doing. The wind catcher about the weather.

I have had only one Idea which is the From a School book . I thought For a moment

My brief is to make a wind catcher. It will be made with wood a plastic bottle and metal Rods and wheels . It works by the hands and wheels . When it is windy the hands go ound and the wind catcher starts to move.

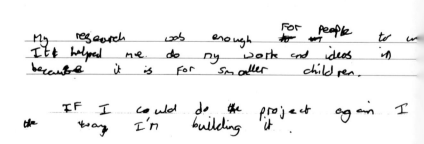

My research was enough For people to u Itt helped me do my work and ideas in because it is For smaller children.

IF I could do the project again I the way I'm building it .

thought a wind catcher
5-7 year olds to learn

her I had this Idea
then decided to do it.

I ~~do~~ Found my answer in a book called Projects in c.d.c.
I chose the windcatcher because I thought it would help the 5-7
year olds learn about the weather.
It helped me choose the idea for the small children to learn
about the weather.

Wind catcher
It works

~~The~~ The decision ~~I~~ I have to make is to see how I am going
~~to get the hand~~ head rods in side ~~the~~ ~~plastic bottle~~ bottle
It is important to get it right because if it does not go right.
the windcatcher will not move so it has to be right to make
the hands go round and so that ~~the~~ the wind catcher
moves.

Way

change

GARETH

At first sight this looks like a high-powered project, but a closer study shows that this able pupil is not demonstrating a particularly high capability, even if the work is impressive. Confident and expressive use of language and graphics illustrates an ability to reflect in some detail. Yet this reflection, being mainly theoretical, is separate from action, rather than influencing actions taken.

Gareth took the opportunity of using this project to explore technical matters which interest him, i.e., he is doing an electronics project. This is not necessarily the same as using electronics as a resource for d&t activity. High-tec reflective work, including mechanisms and electronics, gives the illusion of being active, when it is theoretical.

If Gareth had tested his ideas using prototypes, and linked the ideas with issues, e.g. who will use it and how it will be used, then he might have worked with a more appropriate balance of the active and reflective aspects, confronting each of them in a concrete and practical way as he developed his ideas.

You don't want to demotivate an enthusiastic individual. How could you keep his or her motivation whilst broadening the considerations the pupil actively confronts?

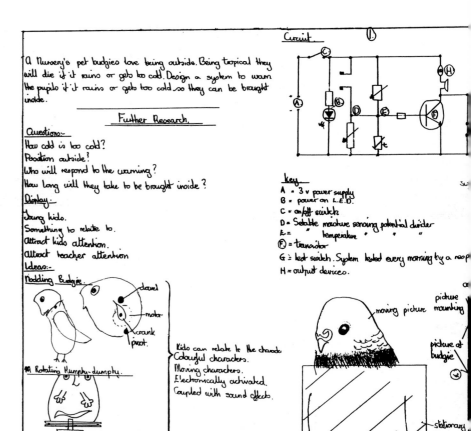

My project is progressing well. I am well ahead of time which allowed me to add more detail and correct errors more fully in my work. The only real decision left is on which construction method to use e.g. Vacuum forming or acrylic bending the weather cover. I must still decide on the display picture design as it must look effective and recognisable without being too complicated for the children to understand. The decisions left to me do not directly affect the working of the project but only the time taken to build it. Do I go for the quick but more risky method or take longer but be sure of success?

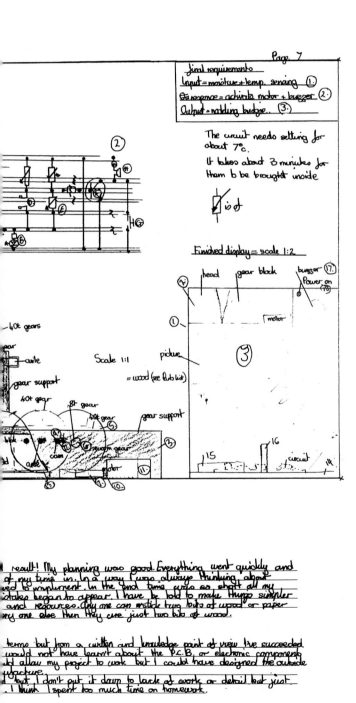

Page 7

Final requirements
Input = moisture + temp. sensing (1.)
Presence = activate motor + buzzer (2.)
Output = nodding budgie. (3.)

The circuit needs setting for about 7°c.

It takes about 3 minutes for them to be brought inside

Finished display = scale 1:2

Scale 1:1

picture
= wood (see Pats list)

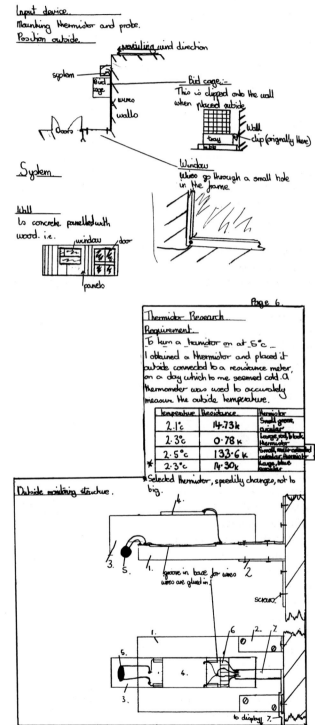

Input device.
Mounting thermistor and probe.
Position outside.

prevailing wind direction

system

Bird cage:-
This is clipped onto the wall when placed outside

wires
walls

doors

Wall
clip (originally Here)

Window
Wires go through a small hole in the frame

System

Wall
Is concrete panelled with wood. i.e.

window   door

panels

Page 6.

Thermistor Research

Requirement
To turn a thermistor on at 6°c
I obtained a thermistor and placed it outside connected to a resistance meter, on a day which to me seemed cold. A thermometer was used to accurately measure the outside temperature.

Temperature	Resistance	Thermistor
2.1°c	14.73k	Small green, circular
2.3°c	0.78k	Large, stud, black thermistor
2.5°c	133.6k	Small, multi-coloured circular, thermistor
* 2.3°c	14.30k	Large, blue thermistor

* Selected thermistor, speedily changes, not to big.

Outside monitoring structure.

groove in base for wires
wires are glued in

screws

to display 7.

result! My planning was good. Everything went quickly and of my time in. In a way I was always thinking about ...ved to implement. In the end time runs as what all my ...stakes began to appear. I have to told to make things simpler and resources. Any one can inside turn bits of wood or paper ...ny one else then they are just two bits of wood.

...terms but from a written and knowledge point of view I've succeeded ...would not have learnt about the P.C.B. or electronic components ...it allow my project to work but I could have designed the outside ...ructure.
...but I don't put it down to lack of work or detail but just ...I think I spent too much time on homework.

KAY

Kay's obvious ability enables her to come up with complex styling ideas, which she reflects on and considers in detail. However, these are not realized as the project proceeds because she lacks the required knowledge and skills (in materials particularly), and she fails to attend to technical and production issues. As a result she eventually produces a stripe which is attached to an existing garment rather than anything more demanding. The project does not encourage Kay to demonstrate her potential capability.

It is often assumed that the more open the project's starting point, the greater the freedom for pupils to attain their potential. Arguably the converse is true, i.e. even a capable pupil needs support and guidance in identifying an appropriate brief. Expecting that capable pupils will find their own level can place pupils at a disadvantage.

If the project had been a vehicle for particular aspects of the Programmes of Study, then learning and progression would have been ensured.

How might you have intervened in the early stages of the project to ensure that Kay chose a brief that would challenge her to pursue new knowledge, skills and understanding?

I am going to design a range of sportswear for sprinting ie. 100m and 200m. indoor and outdoor The coaching centre will be in Southern Britain because we have warm and cold weather there. The clothes will be suitable for men and women of any age but they are for the serious sprinter - not someone who wears it because it is fashionable.

I chose sprinting as the sport I would design clothes for because I think it has a u range of possible designs, for instance, I will not only design clothes for running in, I design sportswear for the athletes to warm up or train in as well. I decided to have coaching centre in Southern Britain because we get a variety of warm and cold weath and I can design clothes suitable for each different weather condition. When I did my res of the history of sprinting sportswear I thought the clothes were unattractive and in cc

I have designed lots of different ideas already, some for indoors, some for outdoors, s training, some for in the rain and some for in hot sunshine. I have used a variety including rubber, glazed lycra, glazed cotton, nylon and a combination of 35% c 65% polyester. Out of those materials glazed lycra and glazed cotton are proba ones most worth using because they are good as they give support, keep you quite reduce sweating and stickiness. Nylon and rubber would not be very good as th uncom

Unfortunately, the school has no Lycra so I will have to material. I will use an equally stretchy material that possible but if it was really manufactored I would use decide how I will print the logo onto the design and is going to be put together to make it possible to be u important to make the right decisions so t

Fabric Qualities

Fabric	Uses in Creative Textiles	Texture and Warmth	Resilience	Absorbency/ Care Label	Strength	Flammable?	Good for Sportswear?	If So What Type?
Cotton	Canvas: rugs, needlepoint calico, drill, sailcloth, repp: background fabrics and household items. Velveteen: cushions, lawn. Cambric: broderie anglais.	Firm, Presses well, Cool to wear.	Poor. Can be stabilised (made crease resistant)	Good Special Finishes	Good, withstands harsh washing. Affected by mildew, acid and sunlight.	Burns readily unless flame-proofed.	Yes	Short-sleeved tops. Jogger Bottoms.
Nylon	Quilting, appliqué blends with other fibres to give strength and better washing qualities	Can be sheer No natural warmth so brushed for warmth	Good	Not absorbent Use antistat "easy care"	Strong, affected by bleach, mineral acid + long sunlight	Does not burn, melts		
Polyester	Quilting, appliqué. Polycotton. Duvet Covers. Quilt wadding.	Wadding filled with trapped air as it is light and warm	Good	Least absorbent, use antistat fabric softener to avoid dirt being picked up	Very strong	Shrinks away from flame, does		
Acrylic	Acrilan, Courtelle: warm and knitted dress fabric suitings. Fleecy Courtelle: dressing gowns. Dralon: curtain fabric	Poor conductor of heat so warm to wear.	Good	Not absorbent "easy care" cold rinse use antistat				
Wool	Coat Weight, Dress Weight Felt, for toys, appliqué etc....	Soft, Warm to wear	Good	Very absorbent				
Silk	Expensive decorative work, ties, cushions, appliqué. Shades...	Soft, luxurious, drapes well. Poor conductor of heat, retains body warmth. Cool for summer.	Good	Absorbent but fine so dries quickly.				

WHAT ATHLETES WORE IN 1920

WHAT ATHLETES WORE IN 1928

WHAT ATHLETES WORE IN 1948

WHAT ATHLETES WEAR TODAY

PROPOSED SOLUTION 3

PROPOSED SOLUTION 2

PROPOSED SOLUTION 1

- Glazed/Shiny Lycra all-in-one body suit, purple with attractive green stripe.
- "Flashback" Logo written down the side
- Tightfitting around the legs, ends just above the knee.
- Purple and green socks.
- "Flashback" trainers

(image: label on suit reads "FLASHBACK")

- All-in-one glazed lycra body suit
- Trainers

(number on suit: 34)

FINAL SOLUTION

- Green stripe made out of stretchy material
- Body suit made out of pink stretchy material. If I could I would have made it purple, but there was no suitable material that was purple.

proto-type of the
...uch like Lycra as
...will have to
... how the design
... a human. It is
... outfit is a success

...my friend, Naomi, lent me a purple all-in-one body suit so all I had to
... cut-out and sew on the Flashback logo down the side of the leg and
...stripe that goes diagonally across the chest. I managed to get the logo
... I still did not have time to do the green stripe. That shows how little
...d. The outfit would have been better if I had used Lycra for the
...he green stripe but the school did not have any green lycra.

...planned the project well but I did not spend enough time making my
...I had, had a few more weeks I think I would have got the results I
...The design I finally chose was difficult to make but I thought I
...able to do it. unfortunately the school had no Lycra and they
...have the right pattern so luckily my friend lent me a body suit
...sed.

SUE

Sue works through the processes of the ATs in that she researched, generated ideas, planned and realized her idea, and evaluated the project. However, doing each Attainment Target in turn is not a good indication of capability, but of separate abilities in some fields.

Sue (like many pupils) thinks that neat work and careful planning indicate capability and that this is what her teacher wants to see. She does not develop and refine her ideas, but thinks that competent practical work and presenting the project well are what's required.

Her aim was to produce a book which helps young children to learn about the weather. Sue's research involved her sister and friends tasting some of the dishes from the book to see if they liked them. Pupils often think that research is simply about asking other people what they think. In this case it would have been more appropriate to evaluate whether young children could use the book successfully and whether it helped them to learn about the weather.

As a desktop publishing exercise this project has merit. Yet technical ability alone is not the same as capability. How could you help pupils to develop this as a resource for capability?

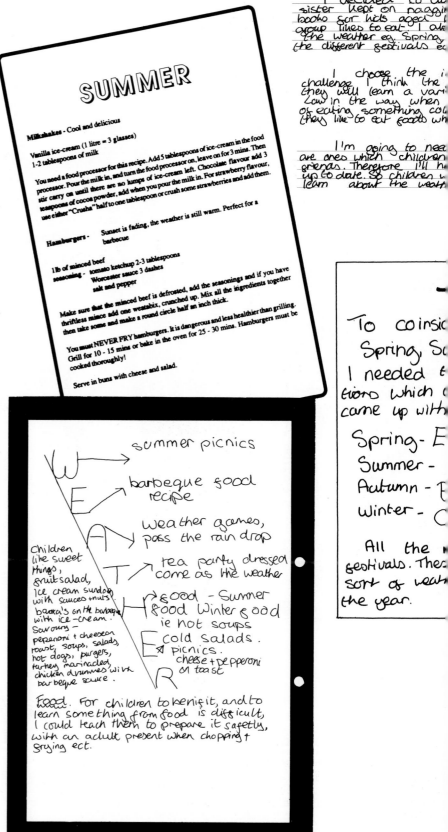

...ather cook book after my little
...to let her cook. But there are no cook
...to my age. Based on what our age
...to link in with my cook book with
...seasons also in the book I will write about
...d the season is Spring.

...cook book, because it is a
...ll benifit alot from my book, and
...kills. They will also learn about murphy's
...in the summer, we automatically think
...salad, and in winter when it is cold
...you up.

...sure that the goods I'm going to make
...t. I will ask my little sister + her
...able source of information which is
...un into reading my book and therefore
...and the different festivals of the year.

...s & Festivals

...h the 4 seasons

...Autumn, Winter.

...os 4 festivals/celebra-
...with all 4 season I

...R

...y (U.S.A)

NIGHT / HALOWEEN

...MAS.

...ill be linked with the
...ls also represent the
...ave at these times of

In My Project

Spring represents - Easter and
shrove Thursday
Summer - barbeques and American
Independence Day
Autumn - Bonfire Night
Winter - Christmas.

The above is what the seasons
linked to the festivals are.

Where do we go got our information:

① Library - children's books. Dewey System.
Reference Section. Metereological information.

② Visit local Schools - Watch children at play / work
Talk to teachers. Look at curriculum.

③ Media Watch - Television: Radio: Newspapers

④ Children and parents - Talk / Discuss and make
notes / record information.

⑤ Reminisce think about own childhood.

⑥ Personal observation of the weather for our project.

How do Children Learn
① By discussion amongst themselves
② By pictures + words.
③ By Observations
④ By touch + play
⑤ By being involved in their own learning.
⑥ Seeing a purpose in what they are doing
⑦ By association - of doing + observing.

My Four Seasons Recipe Book.

The purpose. This will be on what children
eat, at different times of the year. It will
also coincide with the festivals / holidays
during the year ie Easter, Summer Holidays
Halloween + Christmas. It will also include
facts about different vitamins and minerals
they need during the year according to the
weather eg. Summer you eat fresh summer
vegetables. In my recipe book I will try and
teach the following things:
Supervision + safety in the kitchen.
The festivals tied in with that season
and special good eaten

	Savoury	Drink	Dessert
Spring / Easter	Pancakes.	Fresh lemon Juice	Easter Eggs
Autumn	Savoury Baked Potato	Drink Hot Chocolate	Dessert Brownies
Winter Christmas	Savoury Sausage Roll	Drink Eggnog	Dessert Mince Pies

---

Because my research consisted of testing my food on my
little sister + her friends, I think it was enough as Danielles
friends all had different tastes. So I had to include all there
different tastes when I thought of what recipes I was going to
make.

VICKY

Vicky works in an appropriately balanced way, if somewhat below her probable level of capability. This is perhaps an example of a pupil who, given a fairly open starting point to generate ideas from, comes up with something adequate but safe. From this point of view it is not an easy piece of work to assess.

If Vicky had been challenged to work at a higher level of knowledge and understanding from the PoS – for example, by further investigating the properties of suitable materials and testing some alternatives – she would have been capable of fulfilling more advanced demands particularly in terms of construction skills.

However, Vicky is working with a balance of action and reflection in that she reflects on issues, considers them and makes decisions accordingly. Having taken her ideas forward she reflects further as a result, which then informs subsequent action. Action and reflection are, thereby constantly informing one another as ideas are modelled and developed.

To make a reflextive item of clothing to be worn in dangerous weather conditions. Using a fluorescent yellow stripe with a fluorescent orange bears face ~~with attach~~ attached to encourage the child to wear the ~~clothes~~ garment

Agreed brief is:

To make a reflective item of clothing to be worn by a small child in dangerous weather conditions, so they can be ~~seen~~ clearly.

I decided on the design of a bears face on the reflective stripe to encourage the toddler to wear the safety garment. I thought that the bear's face was the best idea, as it was something that many toddlers would recognise. I wanted the garment to be fun, as well as a safety garment.

I did some experiments testing different ways of attaching the material together. I was looking for something that would not show through material, didn't cost much, and was quite easy to do up and un-do. I decided on poppers, even though they showed through the material.

I have not got too much left to do, I have made all my important decisions of what things to use, already, as I carried out experiments, to help me decide. I don't think that I will change much that I have decided on, already. It is important that I get ~~ever~~ everything right as I can't always go back and change it. The game is a safety garment and has to be made properly. The final product has to be safe for a toddler to wear.

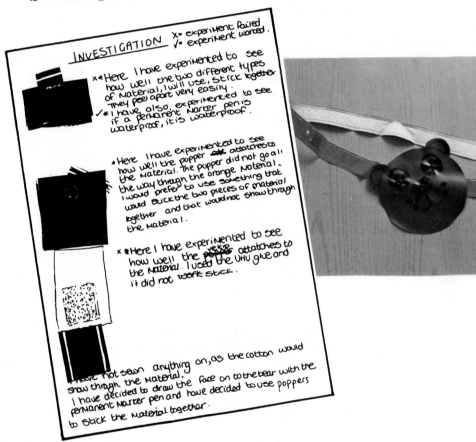

INVESTIGATION X= experiment failed ✓= experiment worked.

X* Here I have experimented to see how well the two different types of material, I will use, stick together. They peel apart very easily.

✓* I have also experimented to see if a permanent marker pen is waterproof, it is waterproof.

* Here I have experimented to see how well the popper ~~sti~~ attaches to the material. The popper did not go all the way through the orange material. I would prefer to use something that would stick the two pieces of material together and that would not show through the material.

X* Here I have experimented to see how well the ~~popper~~ velcro attaches to the material. I used the UHU glue and it did not ~~work~~ stick.

I have not sewn anything on, as the cotton would show through the material. I have decided to draw the face on to the bear with the permanent marker pen and have decided to use poppers to stick the material together.

I have had many ideas of ways of making a bright item of clothing, it could be made as an armband or stripe and to make it more interesting for a toddler (which is the age I'm aiming for) and to encourage them to wear the garment I thought of different ways of presenting it. I thought I could attach some shape to it, a star, a face, some sort of object (also made out of bright material) that the child would like and interests them. So, when they do go out in dangerous conditions, they would want to wear the garment.

The first important decision I would have to make is the design, what I think would interest the child the most. Another important decision would be which fabric is the best to use, which would be the brightest, what would stand out the best in heavy thick fog or bad hail, snow or rain storms. Or if they were out, for some reason, at night what would be the best fabric to wear.

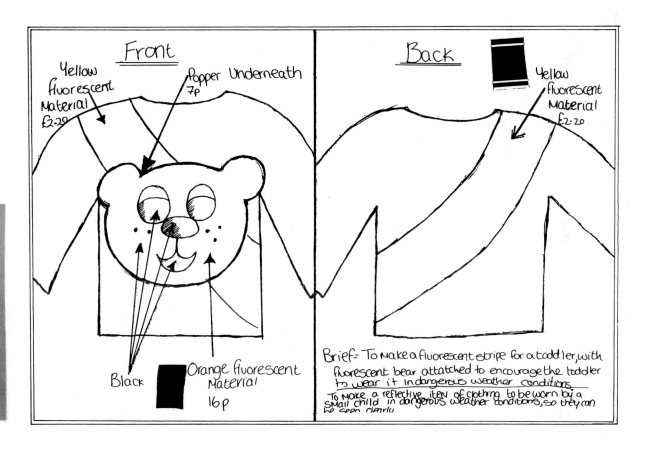

I tried to cater for everything, which, I think, I did. I planned the finish project, what materials to use, what would be the best design, what would the child prefer. I am pleased with the final result, but I'm sure, that if someone else was to look at the finished product they would see something that was wrong with it and how it could be improved.

If I was to do the project again I would do it exactly the same and I wouldn't change a thing. The garment went exactly according to plan, as I planned every step, I found it much easier following a step-to-step guide.

I would use the same plans and make it the same way. I did the right amount of research and planned it well enough, I think. Originally in my plans I had to make some slight changes, but nothing major. Major changes were made.

4 *Assessing Capability*

The context of each project in this chapter needs to be made clear so the reader can consider the project, and the comments made about it, with that awareness. The projects are presented with teacher commentary and assessment notes. We have selected extracts which give a flavour of each project. They were all undertaken by year 9 pupils as part of their d&t school curriculum. They took the form of extended projects which ran over a number of weeks. The teachers involved were, more often than not, planning and running this type of extended d&t project using National Curriculum criteria for the first time. The National Curriculum was in its very early years and was new to teachers and pupils. It presented them with a series of complex demands, unfamiliar working methods and uncertainty about its concepts, let alone how it might best be practised.

The demands of managing and organizing such a project meant that teachers often had little opportunity to evaluate what they and their pupils were doing until it was finished. When they looked back at the experience they could identify many unsatisfactory aspects from which they could learn. Sometimes it was easier for them to see the weaknesses and faults in other teachers' work. Most of their criticisms revolved around their central concern that pupils should be learning and progressing in d&t through appropriate classroom experiences. Looking back they saw that their first attempts were lacking, maybe in the type of starting point that they gave pupils; in the demands made of pupils (or the lack of them); in giving pupils too much or insufficient direction or support, and so on.

We chose these projects because teachers have

found using them invaluable in coming to terms with what d&t is, and how pupils choose to communicate their capability. Teachers considered them to be useful examples of some of the pitfalls and red herrings in assessing capability, and so they serve as a vital resource from which to learn more about how pupils become capable and how teachers might best organize and support that developmental process.

Teachers have said that it was not until they were able to look at the outcomes of pupils' actual activities in d&t that they began to get a feel for capability and how it might be assessed. This is very much the case with d&t itself, it is not until pupils actually try out and test their ideas, that they appreciate what works in reality, and what lessons can be learnt from this.

The teachers who were involved in these projects have since built on these early experiences to further develop the d&t curriculum in their schools, and to include assessment as a purposeful part of that framework. They gained particularly from working with colleagues from different subject backgrounds to their own, to develop shared understandings. The projects have been presented to enable you to work through a similar process.

Teachers often ask whether there is a reliable and valid way of interpreting the Statements of Attainment which is also manageable for the classroom. The key would seem to be to approach the Statements of Attainment in a way which is valid in capability terms - so that it is capability which is being assessed and not just separate skills and unrelated understanding - whilst at the same time guaranteeing reliable and consistent standards between teachers.

Reliable and valid assessments depend on teachers being able to differentiate between capability at each of the ten National Curriculum levels, as well as being able to justify their assessments in fingerprint detail in relation to the SoA.

Teachers have found the following procedure helpful in approaching SoA to make their assessments. You can use this procedure to make your own assessments from the evidence presented in the following projects.

Further activities are suggested in chapter five to enable you to familiarize yourself with National Curriculum assessment and to confront the issues which arise during the process of assessment.

SETTING OUT THE FRAMEWORK

1) Look at the bunches of SoA in the Order across the Attainment Targets at a level to familiarize yourself with what it is that typifies capability at each level - i.e., read the SoA as bunches of criteria which relate to one another, rather than as separate criteria to be separately scrutinised.

2) Reading SoA in this way gives you a level descriptor of capability, and gaining this sense of levelness will help you to see the progression within the Order. Make an initial judgement as to the overall capability level (profile component level) of the work you are assessing. If you are looking at a number of pieces of work, it may help to rank them in overall capability terms, before assigning them to a level. For example, ranking them into piles of work which are demonstrating weak or strong capability, before assigning them to a level.

3) Now that you have found an entry-point for assessment, you need to validate and fine tune your judgements against the SoA for each Attainment Target. Do this by looking across all the SoA which detail capability for the level at which you made your initial professional judgement. For example, if you judge a piece of work to be round about level 4, then look across all the SoA at level 4 to see whether your judgement is borne out through the particular criteria which together describe capability at that level.

4) Which of the SoA can you credit as having been attained? It may be that you do not feel satisfied that the pupil has attained sufficient SoA right across the ATs to be credited at that level. In this case you should look at the SoA for that Attainment Target at the level below, to see if these match the evidence more closely. It may be, however, that you feel that the pupil may be reaching some Attainment Target statements at a higher level than your initial overall judgement. In this case you will want to look to the SoA in the level above to see if enough of these can be credited for that AT.

5) Check against the Programme of Study. Are you satisfied that the pupil is operating with the level of knowledge, skill and understanding represented in the PoS at the level you have judged them to have reached?

So, starting with a 'ball-park' professional judgement (based on a bunch of SoA which taken together describe capability at that level) provides an entry point from which to validate and fine tune your assessment. As such, it provides the detailed SoA and Attainment Target picture of assessment when this is required.

N.B. It should be noted that in making the following assessments, teachers were working with Attainment Targets and Statements of Attainment from the 1990 version of the document *Technology in the National Curriculum*.

WORKING WITH GRAPHIC MATERIALS

LEVEL 3
THEME: WEATHER
CONTEXT: SCHOOL
PROJECT: WEATHER BOOK
PUPIL: JENNIE

Getting started

Aim

To give pupils the opportunity of designing for another person - a young child learning about the weather. Pupils worked on their own but were organized into groups regularly to present and review their work together, sharing ideas and opinions. They were taught about the use of colour and layout.

Assessment 1

There is little evidence of Jennie's exploration of the context. What did she see or find out? She has given some reasons alongside her thinking about how the book should be written and what it should contain. *(Evidence for Tes 1.4a, 1.3b, 2.3e.)*

I am making a book which will explain all about the weather. There will be a cartoon in the book asking the child questions on the subject and explaining about the weather. And in the back of the book will be some games to see how much they have actually learnt.

The thing that made me decide on a would be able to read the words and le pictures that will explain the words if the

This is the only idea I a plain book but if it's wont bother looking at i actually talking to them Et more interesting.

The mar a shorter and also r interest he few games

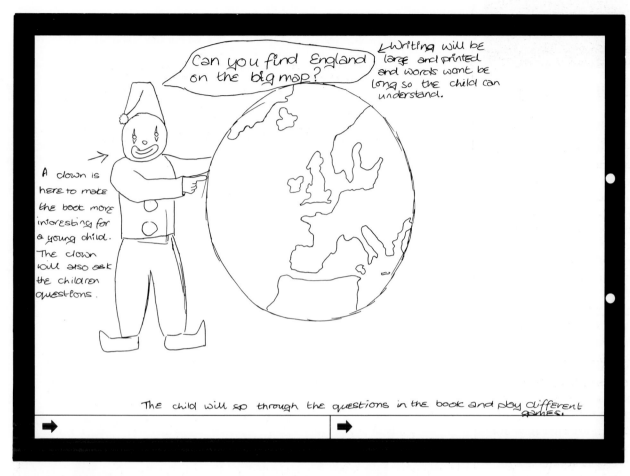

Can you find England on the big map?

Writing will be large and printed and words wont be long so the child can understand.

A clown is here to make the book more interesting for a young child. The clown will also ask the children questions.

The child will go through the questions in the book and play different games.

as the children
m and with
not understood.

ad. At first I was going to make
colourful and interesting children
if there is a cartoon that is
bright and colourful, it might make

om I think, will be putting the long words into
so they can be understood by a young child
ing the book too big that the child will loose
through, and I think this will be helped by a
the way.

The most important decision is the planning and the setting
of the book and not distracting them from the work by
many colourful objects around. And making it interesting
a wide range of age groups.

WORKING WITH GRAPHIC MATERIALS

LEVEL 3
THEME: WEATHER
CONTEXT: SCHOOL
PROJECT: WEATHER BOOK
PUPIL: JENNIE

Developing ideas

Teacher's comments

Jennie worked hard on her project and achieved a lot. She often does not finish her work as she tends to take on too large a task. She has described much of her thinking about the content of the book, but has not covered its graphic presentation as well as I hoped.

Assessment 2

Jennie describes how she is trying to compose text and graphics that will be suitable for the young child and then uses her team for feedback on her work. There is little evidence for her first attempts at this, just the early version of the whole book.
(Evidence for Tes 1.3b, 2.3a, 2.3b, 2.3e, 4.3a.)

I don't think I have learnt much through this project.
I think next time I will do a bit more planning before actualy starting the main thing

It helped to know the sort of things by telling what to write in my book and the child has to know in order to understand. But I don't think it helped all that muc

If I could do the project again I would like to explained about the weather and I would u of the different types of weather on a tape me come up with my ideas was trying it 5, 7, and 10.

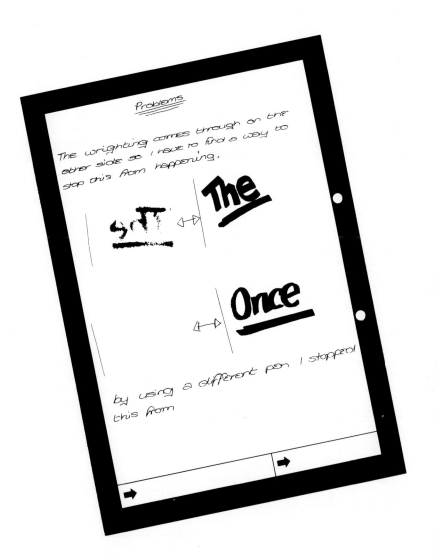

Problems

The wrighting comes through on the other side so I have to find a way to stop this from happening.

SoT ⟷ The

Once

by using a different pen I stopped this from

needed to know
sort of things
weather map.

e the way I
record noises
ing that made
children of

I think the planning helped the final result alot as I wouldn't
ave explained about the weather like that I would have used
ifferent words wich the child would not have understood. If I
one this again I would make Charlie (my clown) into a boy and
ouldn't have made the book so big.

I would make my results better by making the book more
ourfull and having more games and experiments for the child
o do.
I'm not pleased with the result. Its too dull and needs more
olour and Charlie should be in it more and I think the
yout should be changed a little as I don't think it's the kind
of book a child will
see and naturaly be
intorested and want to
pick it up.

WORKING WITH GRAPHIC MATERIALS

LEVEL 3
THEME: WEATHER
CONTEXT: SCHOOL
PROJECT: WEATHER BOOK
PUPIL: JENNIE

Making things happen

Project review

How could Jennie have been encouraged to explore the context and use research techniques? Do you think that the teacher discussed sufficiently the scale of the project with Jennie? How far do you think this qualifies as a genuine d&t project - rather than an English or art project? What teaching on graphic techniques would you have provided?

Assessment 3

Jennie had some trouble realizing her idea, e.g. the pen bled through the paper. There is little evidence of her knowledge and understanding of tools and materials as she mainly used simple pens and paper. Her final review covers her working and the quality of her solution. It would have been good to have some real feedback from 'the child'.
(Evidence for Tes 2.3e, 3.3b, 3.3d, 4.3a, 4.3b.)

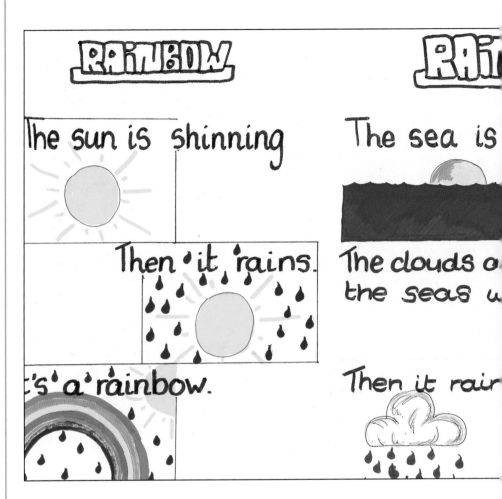

I used what I found out to decide what the young children can and can't understand and how to made it more interesting for them. As having maps with big lines every were will confuse them and having books with small writing and large words they won't understand.

I used the idea I chose because I tried it out on young children of 5/7 and 10 and they chose this idea to be the easiest to understand and more interesting. And they would also like more games and other activitys in the book to do with the weather.

I have made half a book and have now decided to write it out in a different way. So I am planning my new idea. Instead of having on going sentences. I am going to do little sentences and more colourful pictures because pictures seem to tell young children abt more than words.

I have to decide how big this book will be as if I write too much they will get bourd with it half way through. I also have to decide what kind of activitys and games I can put in this book so it is more interesting for them. I have already done a small game but they would like more.

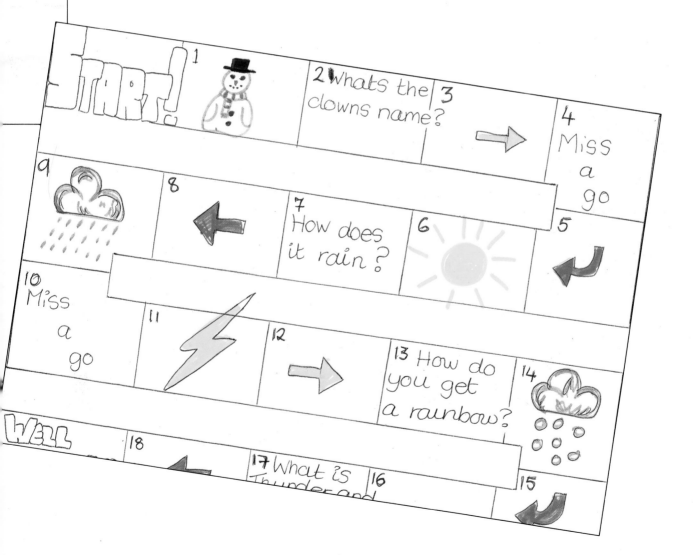

WORKING WITH GRAPHIC MATERIALS

LEVEL 4
THEME: WEATHER
CONTEXT: SCHOOL
PROJECT: TEACHING-AID
PUPIL: PAULA

Getting started

Aim

This group had considerable experience of entire d&t activities focused on realization. The topic and task were structured so pupils could look at aesthetic appeal, changing preferences and human scale. To do this the pupils were given help and support in thinking about ways in which children's interest is used to stimulate learning. A card mechanisms and pop-ups activity was added to the project to encourage pupils to produce more interactive ideas.

Assessment 1

The questions she asked her mother (the teacher) showed she had a good grasp of young children's needs. Her research enabled her to come up with a sensible list of constraints for what her idea must be like and do. *(Evidence for Tes 1.4b, 1.4c, 1.4e, 2.4a.)*

My brief is to make a chart with moveable pieces and brightly coloured parts so that children can learn about the weather.

TASK

Primary school teachers teach their pupils about the weather. Young children are usually interested in things that move and things that they can get involved in. Design and make something that will make learning about the weather fun for young children.

THINK ABOUT

How young children learn

What they may already know about the weather

What they need to know

Movement

Appeal to young children

Durability

Ease of use

Safety

Materials

Methods of construction

Size

Cost

IDEAS: I have h
these ideas

CLIMATES
HOT
COLD
WINDY   SEASON

WINTER
SUMMER
SPRING
AUTUMN

From e
possible ways
interesting way
I could
or a chart ab
in which they
I have
like and dislike
which a child

IDEA'S

I would like to make an item for the ages 4-8 this item could be used for older children with special needs.

From my research I have found that the item needs :-
- To be brightly coloured and eye catching.
- To be something that the child can take part in.
- To make them curious and interested.

You need to take into account :-
- What they already know.
- What they need to know.
- What sort of learning they find interesting.
- What activities they enjoy.
- That it can't be time consuming.

Here are some ideas :-

Put this piece here
Wood
Wood

To learn about the seasons and what the weather is like is one idea.

You turn the wheel to match the season up with the weather. Then you will have small magnetic words saying the weather. Then you can match the words with the season as well.

WINTER SUMMER
AUTUMN SPRING
magnetic pieces
SUN
RAIN SNOW
WIND
magnets

SNOW SUN

SNOW

FOG STO

A Jigsaw which
picture.

I have decided to
with a solution to the p

...eas, before we started. To expand on
...a chart and add more ideas:-

...chart, I have come up with several
...to learn about weather, in a fun and

...o do with countries and their climates,
...can do in certain weather, or a chart
... the day's weather is like.
...I do some research into what children
...there is no point in making an item
...with very quickly.

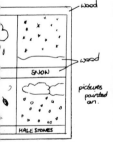

...d or varnished
wood

...he middle, like dominoes

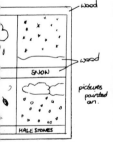

...ut the word with the

...ne and three to come up

RESEARCH

As my mum is a teacher (ages 3 to 5) I decided to interview her on what children like, what they find interesting and wether they react to interesting and brightly coloured things.

QUESTIONS :-

1. What do young children find interesting?
   Because they are young they are curious, but they enjoy using their senses (e.g touch, feel, taste + see + hear) usually.

2. Do they play with a preference to brightly coloured toys?
   Yes they do.

3. Do children like playing with toys that have moveable pieces?
   Yes, things that they can take part in.

4. Do younger children have a level of concentration?
   Depending on the child you can't really answer this question. It depends on the childs intertectual and emotional developement. It also depends on the childs maturity.

5. What is essential for an educational toy?
   If its for a large group of children it has to be large and very eye catching even if its for a small group of children it still has to be large and eye catching. But it helps if there are moveable pieces. So all in all it has to be interesting.

Developing ideas

Teacher's comments

Paula was lucky in involving a teacher (her mother) in thinking about the kinds of materials that young children might find interesting. This allowed Paula to make well-informed choices about her work and achieve a creditable outcome. The main problem in her work is that there was no time to test her learning aid and so her evaluation of her solution in relation to her intentions is a little sketchy.

Assessment 2

Paula's early ideas are evaluated against her constraints and she shows an awareness of existing items on the market. Her chosen idea is developed to include a rotating wheel (after being taught about mechanisms). Paula is able to review her thinking and justify each part of her design in terms of its purpose and appeal. *(Evidence for Tes 1.4d, 2.4a, 2.4b, 2.4d, 3.4e.)*

I have had several ideas for charts. One was where you had a turning wheel split i picture about what you can do in certain weather, e.g. make a snow man. Then round and you would match the pictures on the wheel to the words. Then some magnetic piece chart, and they would have to put the magnetic pieces with the word of weather e.g. S I thought of a match up game of cards where you match the word e.g. snow blu

Problems could be what size to have the chart. Making sure it doesn't come apa going to get the pictures from? I could solve these by experimenting with card h

The size is important as well as bright colours and making it interesting. Hou getting the child interested. Also the time it takes for the activity is important. If it takes interest.

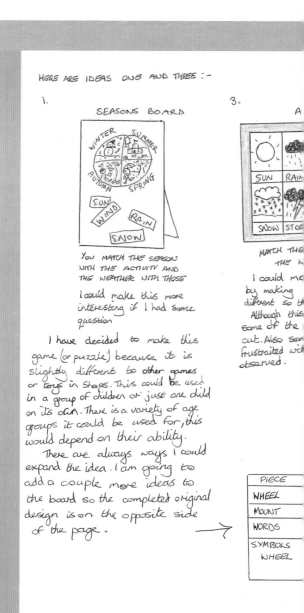

HERE ARE IDEAS ONE AND THREE :-

1.

SEASONS BOARD

You MATCH THE SEASON WITH THE ACTIVITY AND THE WEATHER WITH THOSE

I could make this more interesting if I had some question

I have decided to make this game (or puzzle) because it is slightly different to other games or toys in shops. This could be used in a group of children or just one child on its own. There is a variety of age groups it could be used for, this would depend on their ability.

There are always ways I could expand the idea. I am going to add a couple more ideas to the board so the completed original design is on the opposite side of the page.

3.

MATCH THE THE W

I could ma by making different so th Although this some of the cut. Also som frustrated wi observed.

PIECE
WHEEL
MOUNT
WORDS
SYMBOLS WHEEL

...in each a bright
...here would be the seasons
...scattered around the
...e season.
...e of snow.

...aus but where am I

...are a good help in
...en the child will Coose

I chose to make a puzzle type board instead of a jigsaw because the puzzle or jigsaw would be very time consuming in cutting all the pieces.
I chose to make the puzzle board, because it would be easy to make and I think because it is different to other toys, children would find it more interesting. Also it will be very brightly coloured to help attract the childs intrest.
The board wouldn't be time consuming for the child so the child wouldn't lose intrest as quickly.

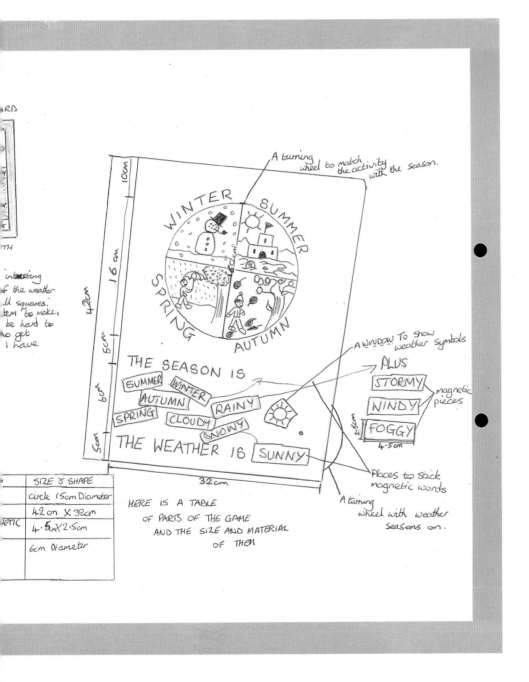

A turning wheel to match the activity with the season.

A WINDOW To show weather symbols

A turning wheel with weather seasons on.

Places to stick magnetic words

HERE IS A TABLE OF PARTS OF THE GAME AND THE SIZE AND MATERIAL OF THEM

SIZE & SHAPE
Circle 15cm Diameter
42cm X 32cm
4·5cm X 2·5cm
6cm Diameter

WORKING WITH GRAPHIC MATERIALS

LEVEL 4
THEME: WEATHER
CONTEXT: SCHOOL
PROJECT: TEACHING AID
PUPIL: PAULA

Making things happen

Project review

What support would you have given Paula in developing her graphic communication skills?
How well do you think she used the materials and knowledge at her disposal?
What methods would you have suggested for evaluating the working and the outcome of this project?
How well do you think Paula used the teaching and learning in this project?

Assessment 3

Paula was quite reflective about what her idea would need to look like and do to be successful, but used fairly limited graphic and production skills and knowledge in achieving her outcome (card, paper fastener, magnets and felt-tip pen). Throughout her project she shows considerable skill in reviewing her working but her final evaluation is limited mainly to her feelings of success in achieving a good-looking outcome.
(Evidence for Tes 2.4b, 3.4d, 4.4a, 4.4b.)

I have learnt that the project I've made can be used for a range of ages depending on the childs ability. I also learn't from a questionari that children like bright colours. Also the attraction of moving parts can help keep the childs attention.

I enjoyed and managed to draw the pictures of each type of weather.

To make things go even better in my next project I will try to expand my ideas and think of improvements before I start.

I did alot of research into my project before I started to des I did a survey into what sort of educational toys teach the the most but in a fun way. To get some of this information I in a school teacher. She teached the ages 4-5. I also watched children at and play to see what they liked and disliked and to see what sort equipment they learnt from.

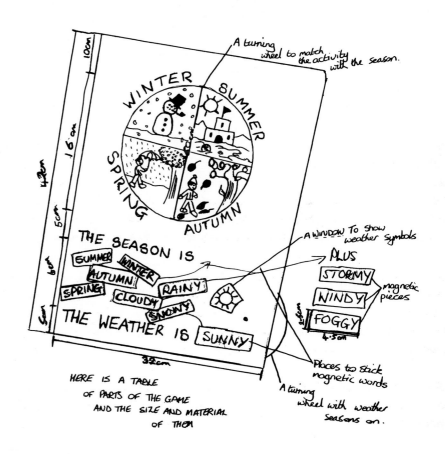

A turning wheel to match the activity with the season.

WINTER
SUMMER
SPRING
AUTUMN

THE SEASON IS
SUMMER WINTER
AUTUMN
SPRING CLOUDY RAINY
SNOWY
THE WEATHER IS SUNNY

A WINDOW To show weather symbols

PLUS
STORMY
WINDY
FOGGY

magnetic pieces

Places to stick magnetic words

A turning wheel with weather seasons on.

HERE IS A TABLE OF PARTS OF THE GAME AND THE SIZE AND MATERIAL OF THEM

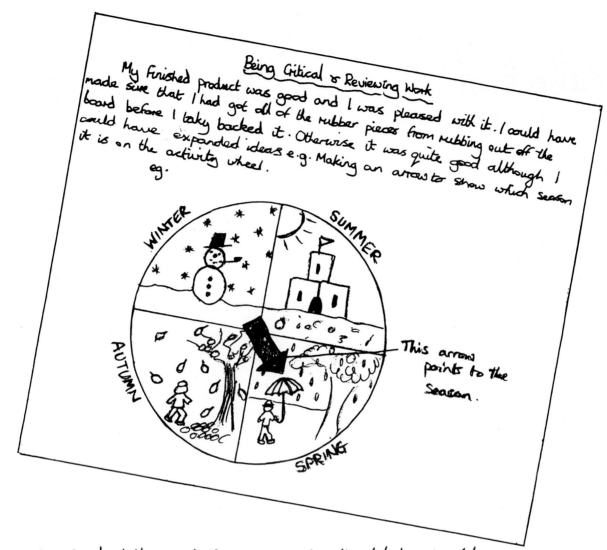

Being Critical & Reviewing Work

My finished product was good and I was pleased with it. I could have made sure that I had got all of the rubber pieces from rubbing out off the board before I tacky backed it. Otherwise it was quite good although I could have expanded ideas e.g. Making an arrow to show which season it is on the activity wheel.

eg.

WINTER
SUMMER
AUTUMN
SPRING

This arrow points to the season.

...m the research I found childrens attention was mostly attracted by colourful ...and moveable pieces. So I set to work to design something on those lines. ... up with several ideas two of them I rejected because they were too ...cated to make in the time we had or that there were many toys like ...t schools in the first place. I developed one idea so it would make it more ...ing. I don't think I would design anything that differently if I had to do it again.

...ning what materials to use was quite difficult but it had to be strong and ...so I used wood in some cases and card to finish it off and make it look nice. ...e cases I decided to tacky back pieces so they didn't get dirty or damaged. ...had to make it again the only thing I'd do differently is when I tacky backed ...n card piece I'd make sure I'd got all the rubber pieces off.

...results were quite good. But I could have expanded my work and make ...row to show which season it is on the big wheel. Otherwise I have finished ...d project.

WORKING WITH GRAPHIC MATERIALS

LEVEL 5
THEME: WEATHER
CONTEXT: SCHOOL
PROJECT: WEATHER MAP
PUPIL: VASHA

Getting started

Aim

This group had considerable experience of d&t tasks. The project was planned to encourage pupils to record the highlights of their activity. Teaching was planned on graphic communication, in particular, for planning and representing the process of making. (Quality in presentation is expected of all work.) To ensure that pupils justified their decisions and actions, regular review points or tutorials were built into the time structure.

Assessment 1

Vasha shows evidence of research into existing artefacts and professional opinions about the context. She presents her thinking well, referring to a range of issues to consider in her ideas. Her task is specific enough to allow her to develop several possibilities for the appearance and functioning of her idea. *(Evidence of Tes 1.5a, 1.5b, 2.5c.)*

I have had many ideas during this project and I like most of them about the good and bad things about them eg. will an idea take too be too complicated or fragile, will it be durable and safe as that is have to consider . . . are my ideas to boring or so easy for the educate them any more. one of my ideas is to make a [cut] out of w with green felt, then make symbols with material to stick on the [co]

. . . of [li]
. . . that
. . . and
. . . give
. . . educ

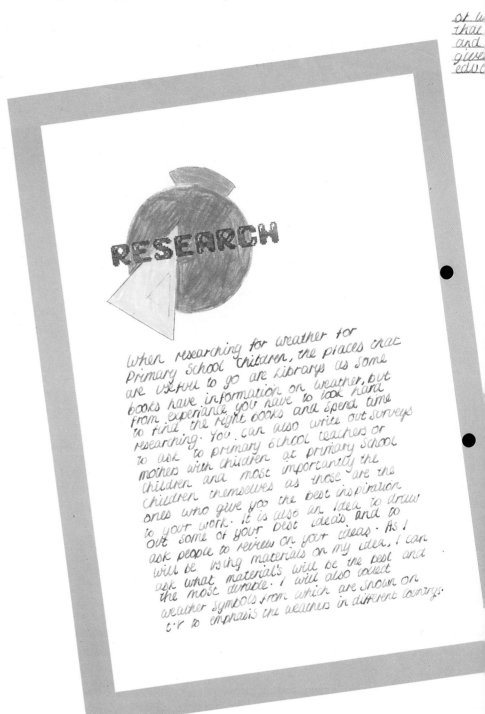

RESEARCH

When researching for weather for Primary School children, the places that are useful to go are Librarys as some books have information on weather, but from experiance you have to look hard to find the right books and spend time researching. You can also write out surveys to ask to primary school teachers or mothers with children at primary school children and most importantly the children themselves as those are the ones who give you the best inspiration to your work. It is also an idea to draw out some of your best idea's and to ask people to review on your idea. As I will be using materials on my idea, I can ask what materials will be the best and the most durable. I will also collect weather symbols from which are shown on t·r to emphasis the weathers in different countrys.

have to think
make, will it
the main facts you
and will it not
Europe, cover it
the appropriate kind

will pick the ideas
exciting, and easy
make in the time
which one will
the most

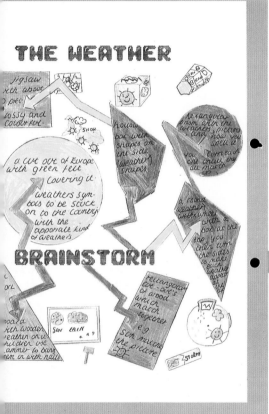

THE WEATHER

BRAINSTORM

jigsaw
rich about
a piece
glossy and
colourful

a cut out of Europe
with green felt
covering it

weathers sym-
bols to be stuck
on to the country
with the
appropriate kind
of weather

house
box with
shapes on
the side
(weather)
shapes

rectangular
foam with the
weather picture
and how you
spell it
you turn read
one until they
all match

SUN RAIN

board
with wooden
weather on it
children use
hammer to bang
them in with nails

a rainy
weather
wheel with a
box at the
top you
then turn
the sides
to make
each
weather
appear
one
by one

rectangular
cut-outs
of wood
which
match
together
e.g.
SUN RAIN
the picture

STORM

this weather symbol
means it will be cloudy
but warm and some sun-
shine

this symbol is very obvious
and means that is that
area there will be lots
sunshine.

this symbol means it
will be dark and cloudy
with rain

again this symbol is
obvious and means that
there will be thunder
and lightening

this means it will be dark
and cloudy.

5. Do you think these toys around
at the moment are useful or not?

- the ones I have seen all seem to
be involved to young children like
toddlers.

6. Do you think these toys really emphasis
the real facts about the weather?

- no, there very basic.

7. Do you think there should be more toys
on the market about the weather?

- yes definately the quicker the better.

8. What age do you think children should
know about the weather -?

- 6

9. Does your child know what the weather
is like in different countries?

- no

10. Does he know what animals like in
different countries?

- no

11. As there is a gap in the toy manufacturing market on toys. do you think
it should be filled?

- Yes as children dont really know
enough about the weather, from the

questions that you have
asked me.

An interview with a mother who has a child in primary school.

1. How old was your child when he
learnt about weathers?

- he was about 5-6.

2. Does he still remember about them?

- Occasionally.

3. Does he ever talk about the things
he has played or done in school
to you.?

- yes, and will go into detail with
it, if he really enjoyed playing with
it

4. Does you child have any toys that
help him learn about the weather?

- No, there doesnt seem to be many
around

WORKING WITH GRAPHIC MATERIALS

LEVEL 5
THEME: WEATHER
CONTEXT: SCHOOL
PROJECT: WEATHER MAP
PUPIL: VASHA

Developing ideas

Teacher's comments

Vasha produced a very thorough and well-presented project. She recorded her decisions and justified her actions in terms of the needs she identified from the context. She has not recorded some of the thinking and learning she undertook in relation to the graphic and textile materials she used. In future projects I want Vasha to develop more complex ideas, perhaps in three dimensions or involving interconnecting or moving parts.

Assessment 2

Pupils often produce different solutions rather than developing aspects or variations of one potential solution, as Vasha has done. She used her experience to sketch the production of her idea, allowing her to identify where decisions still need to be made.
(Evidence of Tes 2.5a, 2.6b, 2.5c, 2.5d, 2.5e, 3.5a.)

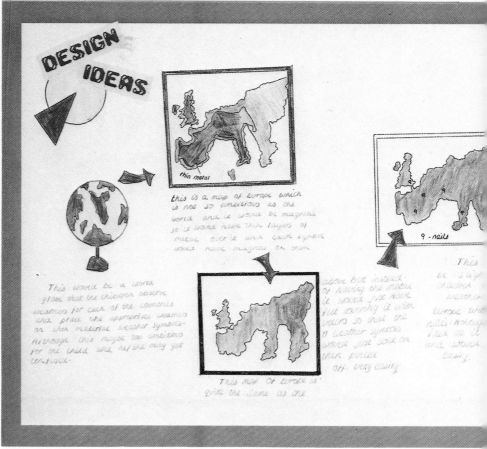

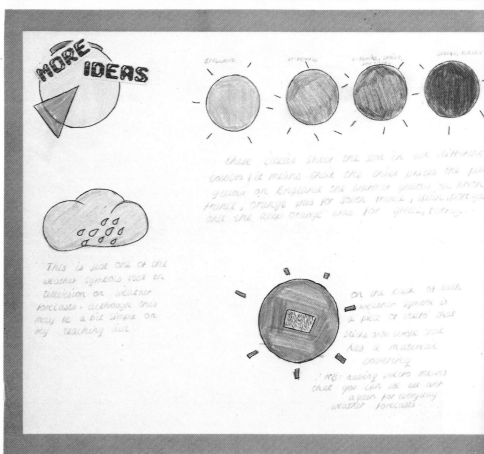

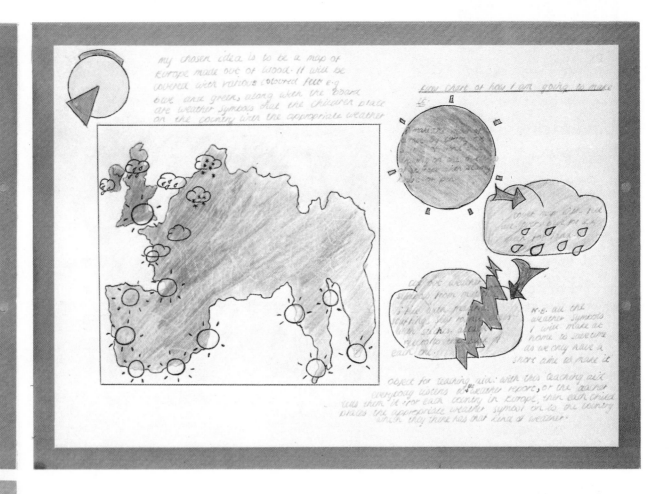

I decided on my brief as the context was to make something interesting and fun but educational for children to learn them about the weather. When I make my toy I will have to think on what children like to play with, they like bright mobile things which you can use again, they also like toys that they can show that they have done something to their parents or teachers and be proud of it. I would also have to think about how strong it will be as children are fairly rough with toys and occasionally throw them about.

The main problems I may come across in this project is if my idea is taking too long to make so I will have to plan ahead, step by step what I will be making in school and what I can make at home. I will also have to consider wether my idea will be too complicated to make so I will deal with this by asking different people's opinions on my ideas as then they will be viewed in different aspects, I also have to think whether my idea is educational as that is the real reason we.

To make my project be a success, I will have to stick to the task frame given and to make my idea based on that text and is not change my mind and make completely different which doesn't relate to the project at all, I will have to consider what materials I be intending to use be available and in fact make my whole idea, safe, durable, educational yet fun to play with for primary school children.

WORKING WITH GRAPHIC MATERIALS

LEVEL 5
THEME: WEATHER
CONTEXT: SCHOOL
PROJECT: WEATHER MAP
PUPIL: VASHA

Making things happen

Project review

How would you have intervened so Vasha was stretched to tackle a more complex idea?

What aspects of knowledge and understanding about materials would you have expected to see in a project using mainly graphic media?

How could you have structured this project to ensure that pupils developed a means of testing their outcomes?

Where do you feel Vasha is weakest and what would you do to ensure that she progressed?

Assessment 3

Vasha's work focused on the success of her design in relation to the needs she identified, rather than the solution's production, maybe because it was relatively simple to construct. She continuously reviewed her work during the project and was able to use her original intentions as criteria for evaluating the success of her outcome. *(Evidence of Tes 2.5e, 3.5a, 3.5b, 3.5c, 3.5d, 4.5a, 4.5b.)*

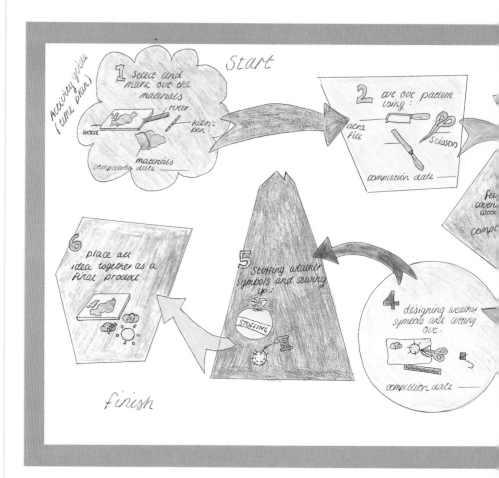

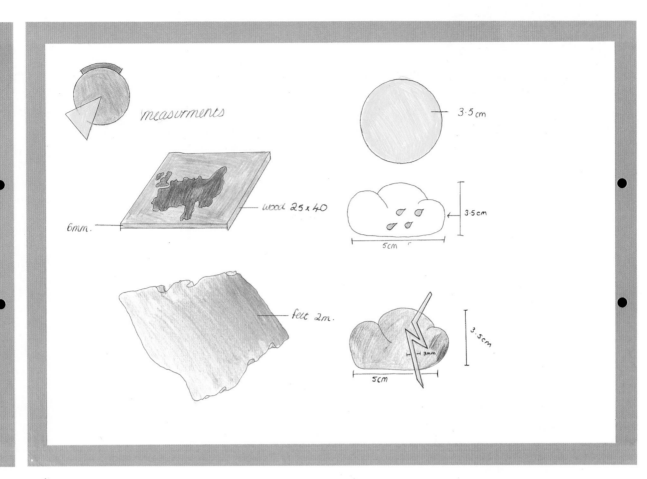

measurments

3·5 cm

wood 25 x 40

6mm.

felt 2m.

3.5cm

5cm

3.5cm

3mm

5cm

idea I am going
to make mine
this ones especially
make my attachments
cloth materials
they will all be

and it is not
so that they are
is a safe material
the the aims

I have learnt quite alot on this D.T
project because I have found out that
there are not many games around which
help children (I learnt about the weather) I learnt to research on my
projects which e.g mean are going to
library's to look things up.
I like actually making things in D.T
rather than doing persective drawings
e.t.c as I find them a little confusing.
To make my project even better next
time I would prefer more time to think of
ideas and to ask people there views on
my ideas

way I wanted to as I made sure I wouldn't change
as making it I did decide on different weather
more attractive and bright. I did get the
working mostly in control e.g (by hand) and I only
it. If I did it again maybe I would change
instead of felt and add lights e.t.c.

have done. I think I stuck to my original idea
and I think it has turned out well. I like
to my ideas. I never thought I would end up
my projects better. I think I would of needed extra
had more graphics and ages to my work. I also
judgements on my ideas then I would be able to

WORKING WITH FOOD
MATERIALS

LEVEL 3
THEME: WEATHER
CONTEXT: SCHOOL
PROJECT: CLOUD COOKIES
PUPIL: BEN

Getting started

Aim

To introduce pupils to looking at food from an aesthetic or visual point of view by depicting the weather. Pupils are given some freedom in the kind of food they produce but through discussion are limited to the more visual forms of food (cakes, biscuits, pizza, flans). The context was intended to be 'unfamiliar' (for achievement at level 4 and above).

Assessment 1

Ben has not really explored an unfamiliar context - he has just made guesses about what 8-9 year olds might be doing. He had several ideas and gave simple reasons for each of them guided by his experience of food.
(Evidence for Tes 1.3a, 1.3b, 2.3e.)

My brief is to design something that's to do with the weather and is going to be exciting and easy for a child to make

What I Lear

I learned abo
explained thin
would enjoy r
such a way t
getting involved
Primary School
of some sort o

I am going to loc
work with,

CLIMATE
AND
WEATHER
Laurie Bolwell
Clifford Lines

Today I learned about how young children aged 3-4 years old were taught. I looked at books which explained things to children of that age. These books are designed in such a way that the children would enjoy reading them. I also saw a video. In this video was Nursery children working in such a way that they really enjoy it. The video showed children looking at colourful pictures and getting involved in these things so they really enjoy learning about these things.

...ach their pupils about the weather. As you know young children are usually more ...at move and things that they can get involved in. What ideas could make ...weather fun for very young children?

...young children aged 3-4 yrs old were taught. I looked at books which ...dren of that age. These books are designed in such a way that the children ...em. I also saw a video. In this video were Nursery children looking at colourful pictures and ...enjoyed it. The video showed children looking at these things. When I was in ...things. So they really enjoy learning about weather through a weather chart. We would put a picture ...ned about weather through a weather chart. ...er in that day on the chart.

...mething for 8-9 yr olds which would make weather sound great to

...e the
...books
...dren
...ram
...nt

I am going to look at making food to teach about the weather. I have chosen the age group 8-9 because they will probably be working with kitchen utensils and a cooker.

Ideas

Book

WEATHER

WORKING WITH FOOD MATERIALS

LEVEL 3
THEME: WEATHER
CONTEXT: SCHOOL
PROJECT: CLOUD COOKIES
PUPIL: BEN

Developing ideas

Teacher's comments

Ben is a careful pupil who likes to get on with making his idea as quickly as possible. In this project he was encouraged to come up with more than one idea and was given support in choosing an appropriate idea to develop. He was able to use his skill in making to produce both a template/cutter and later a box. However, he didn't think very much about how his idea would be suitable for teaching pupils about the weather.

Assessment 2

Ben recorded lots of practical activity on how he was producing his idea. He did not record his development thinking in working out how to make his biscuit look like a cloud, just a 'final solution'. This is fairly typical of level 3 - lots of 'what I am doing' and 'how I am doing it', less of the 'why it has to be like that'. *(Evidence of Tes 2.3a , 2.3b, 2.3d, 2.3e, 3.2b, 3.3c, 3.3d.)*

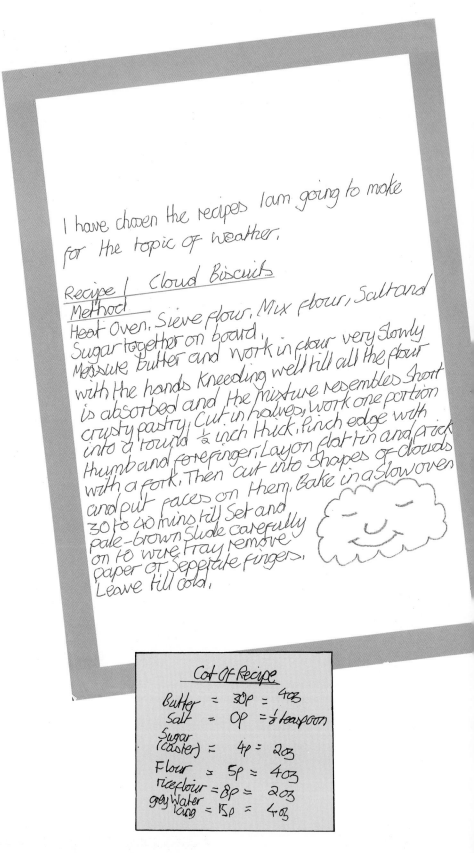

Plan Of Action
1. Decide on recipies,
2. Make the templates,
3. Test recipe and templates to see if they work, won't

Cutter

This is used to make the shape of the Cloud Biscuits

How to Make Cutter
1. Get a Strip of card
2. Put the ends of the strip together and cellotape them together,
3. Then put cellotape around the whole of the card. Make sure the whole card is covered with cellotape inside and outside,
4. Then bend the card into a shape of a cloud,

This is the shape of the cutter I made.

Ingredients
Butter
Salt
Caster Sugar
Flour
Plain Flour
a teaspoon of baking
Currants

WORKING WITH FOOD MATERIALS

LEVEL 3
THEME: WEATHER
CONTEXT: SCHOOL
PROJECT: CLOUD COOKIES
PUPIL: BEN

Making things happen

Project review

How could Ben have been encouraged to explore the context?

How well do you think this project works using food as a material?

How can pupils be enabled to be more inventive and creative with food than merely choosing a recipe?

What teaching would you include in this project to help Ben build on his knowledge and understanding?

Assessment 3

Ben made references to what children would find 'easy' and 'fun' in justifying his ideas and decisions. He recounted the problems he had with the shortness of the biscuit mixture and the box initially being too small. His evaluation is based on his subjective experience of his own actions - rather than linking them to any constraints or issues identified for his idea - typical of level 3.
(Evidence for Tes 3.3d, 4.3a, 4.3b.)

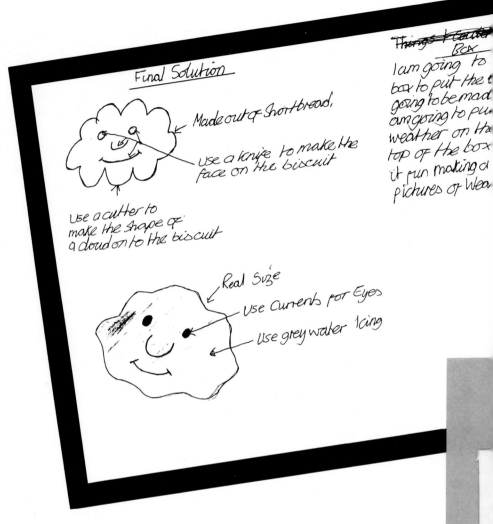

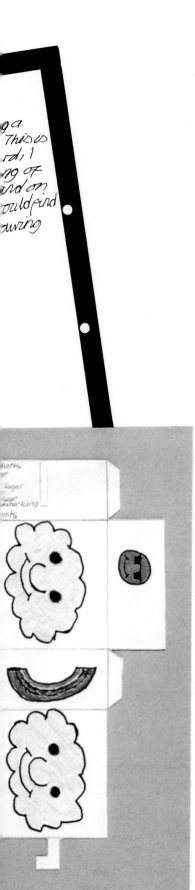

g a
This is
rd, I
ng of
nd on
ould find
awing

Evaluation

Biscuit :- It turned out well in size, colour, texture, - taste was lovely. Cutting the shapes, and then picking up the biscuits was difficult because they could easily break. They were easy to identify than because the shape and colour, were exactly right, improvements what needed. I had to improve the amount - of butter, I didn't bring enough. I quite enjoyed the research and making the biscuits. It was interesting to know how children think and enjoy making some items. When I took it home, the family liked it. I think if children work with such ideas they going to find it fun and interesting to work with such ideas.

Box :- The problem with this, was the box was to small so I made another. The material was great for the biscuits. The box was made of card. To do the lettering on the box I could have used a stensy. I used felt tip pen to draw clouds on the box. This would be fun for a child to draw a clouds on the box. Little children find it fur more fun to work with paint when drawing.

What I enjoyed and didn't enjoy in the whole project

I liked looking at the video and books to see how children would work and read. This way I could work out how to make something children would enjoy working with. I also enjoyed making the biscuits. I didn't enjoy the review sheets I found the questions hard, some didn't make sense to me.

Problems

I had two problems!
1) I didn't have enough butter, I needed more than what was on my recipe. To avoid this you must bring a little bit more.
2) Cutting the shapes they break easily - you must be careful

WORKING WITH FOOD MATERIALS

LEVEL 4
THEME: ON THE MOVE
CONTEXT: RECREATION
PROJECT: FOOD FOR A DAY TRIP
PUPIL: MANI

Getting started

Aim

To teach pupils more about the nutritional value of foods and how to make realistic costings. The starting point was to think about food needed for a journey including food for a person with special dietary needs. Pupils will learn about meeting different dietary needs and be encouraged to think about interesting and unusual solutions.

Assessment 1

Mani has thought hard about what might be possible and likely in planning her trip. This seems to have been based on experience and common sense. Later she found a 'disabled' person and explored their particular needs - though not much of this information has been recorded.
(Evidence for Tes 1.4a, 1.4b, 1.4c, 1.4e, 2.4c.)

p to London. I will
the disabeled or
we will be travelling
don by train. We
holidays, when the
y We will be visiting* and
shopping.
(*museums)

the reason, I chose my brief was because it seemed like a challenge. Most people
h group decided to do sports. So I thought I'd be different. Everyone else just
ke care of themselves, where as with mine I have to think about other people.
of other people is not always easy, so that's why I chose it. I also
t other people then decided to do a similar choice to me. I also chose to
because I wanted to help other people, help them get out and enjoy themselves.

eas I have had are to take the food with me. Making sure that it is
operly, according to the weather. Also to make sure there are toilets for
eople. Also if the weather is cold, there should be hot meals available in
restaurants. If the weather is extremly bad, I'll need waterproofs, to protect
ll also take money to enter museums, camera's, paper to draw sketches. I dont
ed to worry about it snowing, because we are going in the summer time. However
ther is hot, I'll need to concentrate on storage of the food. All the ideas here, I'm going to
in my project. Because these are the important ones, and the first ones that came

think my biggest problem will be the weather. The weather changes from day to day that
so hard to know what I'm going to have to do. To deal with the weather problem,
need to take protective clothing, special storange incease the food turns bad, also
amount of money I'm going to take. I'll also need to know if the disabled person has
cial medication, or is on a special diet. If the underground is closed for some
ason, I might have to seek other means of transport, it dephends.

most important decisions that I'll have to make, is to. a) Chose a person who is
ing to help me take the disabled person out. Also I have to choose to visit
useums and shops, that I think other people will like. I have to choose appropriate
d, incase someone is diabetic, vegeterian or has any special needs. I have to be
ganized, quick to make decisions and know exactly what I'm doing. I have to know
at time were leaving, when were leaving. Also what to do in an emergency.

WORKING WITH FOOD MATERIALS

LEVEL 4
THEME: ON THE MOVE
CONTEXT: RECREATION
PROJECT: FOOD FOR A DAY TRIP
PUPIL: MANI

Developing ideas

Teacher's comments

Mani worked very hard and produced a well-presented solution to her task. She enjoyed her work and this shows in the amount of effort she has put into reporting what she achieved. I was disappointed that she did not include any evidence of what she found out from the 'arthritis person', though this was discussed and used when selecting food for the journey.

Assessment 2

The middle phase of this project was further trials and investigation into possible foods and menus to find an appropriate combination that would be nutritionally satisfactory and sufficiently portable. Mani did not record much about her difficulties in making her dishes.
(Evidence of Tes 2.4a, 2.4b, 2.4c, 3.4a, 3.4b, 3.4c.)

Practical - Lunch and snacks.

... make 3 different sandwiches to fit the people's need. Tuna and cucumber for the arthritis
...lad, for me, and ham salade for my friend. Drinks - will be as follows. Pineapple juice for
...Soda water for arthritis person. I will have fruit and coleslaw and chocolat on display, along
...
...hands put on apron.

Coleslaw. Wash all the veg, you want to put in it. Eg. onion, carrot.
then cut up the onion very finely and grate the carrot. Add a little salt,
and add 2 or more table spoons of mayonnaise. Mix together - and voila!

...salad, leave to dry
...margarine breads.   Nutritional value.
...sandwiches.   Bread: Ingredients Brown flour, water, yeast, salt, vegetable fat, soya flour,
...food for coleslaw.   Emulsifier, E472(e) preservative E282, Dried glucose, syrup. flour, improver E300
...vegetables   Energy 960kj (For 100g). 226kcal. Protein 9.8g. Corbohydrate 44.1g (of which
...mayonnaise.   sugars) 2.5g. Fat 2.3g. (of which saturates) 0.7g. Sodium 0.5g. Dietry Fibre
...bowl.   5.9g.
...display.   Vitamins = thiamin 0.34mg. calcium 6500mg. iron 2.60mg.
...and evaluate.   Cucumber: 95.6g water. 50kj. 13kilocalories. 0.8g protein. 0.1g total liquid fat.
...bohydrate. 30ug A retional equivalents. D (ug) cholecalciferol, 0B thiamin(mg) 0.04 B2-Riboflavin. 0.05mg.
...ents 100g free folic acids, asscorbic acid 8mg. 25mg Ca calcium. 1.1mg fe iron.
...water. 60kj. 14kilocalories. 1.3g protein. 0.2g total liquid fat 97ug A retional equivalents. 0.06mg B12
...B2 Riboflavin. 0.3mg Niconnic acid equivalents. 24ug free folic acids. 8mg casocorbic acid. 35mg
...ng iron.
...per 100g. Energy 155k. protein 1.3g. corbohydrate 4.8g. Total fat 14.7g. Polyunsaturates 4.6g. Saturates 11g.
...0.7g (Ham- (meat) is the same equivelant value)

crisps - per packet.
Energy kj	660 [5]
Protein	1.0 g.
carbohydrate	16.0g.
Fat	9.8g.

tuna ←

Nutritional value of evening meal.

Potatoes : 0.76 protein g/p. Energy = 135kj /p. Vit C. = 5mg/p. 1.5kg provide carbohydrates and some
vitamins.

carrots : 0.26 protein g/p. Energy = 36kj/p. Vit c. = 2mg/p. Plus vit A. - repairs and good vision.

Lamb : protein 0.57g/p. Energy 49 kj/p. Iron 0.024mg/p. Thiamin 0.02 mg/p. Riboflavin mg/p=0.005
Nicotin 0.25 mg/p. B_1 - appetite blood. circulation, energy. growth digestion. B_3 circulation
cholestral reduction, growth, metabolism, protein, fat calcium.

Inositol are in all vegetables. They contain cholestral reductions, slowing down hardening
of the arteries.

Cost of meal
lamb	45		91
peas	9		×3
carrots	7		
potatoes	30		£2.73 ~ evening meal for 3 people.
	91 p per person		

Evaluation. I enjoyed cooking the evening meal, I enjoyed it because it was a relaxing lesson. I
didn't have to rush it, so that I could leave the
lesson on time. I learnt alot from the lesson, for
example, I learnt how to present my work, and
how to cook different foods at the same time. I
managed to help others, and I liked the people
I worked with. If I could change that lesson,
I wouldn't change a single thing, I worked
well and I enjoyed myself. Because of my brief.
I had to make a meal for on arthritis person.
After alot of thought, I managed to make a
meal that all 3 people could eat. I was pleased
with my end result. Also other people liked it, and the
meal looked tasty, healthy and mouthwatering !!!!!!!!!!!!

Method: + Wash hands and put on an apron 10:15am
+ Collect equipment. ————————→ ′′
+ Peel and wash vegetables. ————→ 10:20am
+ Warm up grill. ————————→ ′′′
+ Put meat in the grill ————————→ 10:25am
+ Boil vegetables. ————————→ 10:30am.
+ turn the grill (the lamb over) ———→ 10:40am.
+ Serve on plate and make gravy. ——→ 10:50am.
+ Present to the teacher, and photograph.—→ 10:55am.
+ Wash up, and evaluate. ————————→ 11:05am.
Plenty of time to spare.

WORKING WITH FOOD
MATERIALS

LEVEL 4
THEME: ON THE MOVE
CONTEXT: RECREATION
PROJECT: FOOD FOR A DAY TRIP
PUPIL: MANI

Making things happen

Project review

How could Mani have been encouraged to make a fuller evaluation of her outcome?

Where would you have intervened in this project to ensure that pupils tackled a variety a ways of meeting dietary needs?

How successfully did Mani use the nutritional data she collected?

What teaching would have enabled Mani to progress in demonstrating her capability?

Assessment 3

Mani gives much evidence of what she learnt during her work and the pleasure she had in achieving so much in a short space of time. What is missing is an evaluation of the appropriateness of the 'food for the day trip' from the travellers' perspective. *(Evidence for Tes 2.4c, 3.4a, 4.4a, 4.4b, 4.4c.)*

<u>Evaluation</u>: I really enjoyed doing that practical, for a number of reasons. fi quickly and efficiently. Even though I've made coleslaw and sandwiches many I had to present my work, so I had to make sure that it looked my brief, which I think I did. Even though I will be travelling, I plates. I did this because it looked nicer, however I displayed the carried in, on the photograph. The part I most enjoyed was disp arranging the food, to make it look appealing to eat. I used all knew exactly what I would need because I have made this ty I think that my food, was right for the occasion. The salade appealing in the hot weather. I had to think very carefully, what for the arthritis person. I didn't want to have a hot drink becaus So after alot of thought, I came up with soda water. I chose added preservatives. However there is some fruit available for the Very hard about my display. I included the bags in which to s in which the food will be stored. I also included the travel tick I also included a personal stereo, something to listen to on the Pleased with my result, I took lots of photographs, I only "come out clearly".
I felt very pleased with my end result. I worked with in th quickly. but most of all, I enjoyed it!

Research includes:
Shop's prices.
talking to people who have arthritis.
Books on arthritis
Nutritional value info-books.

worked
was different.
to satisfy
work on
it will be
ork. I liked
pment, I
any times.
ll be most
could have
weather.
se it has no
on. I thought
. The container
ith my purse.
s very
they will
I worked

I have learnt the needs of arthritis people, and what they can and can't eat. I have learnt how to portion food correctly, and how to present the food I make. I have also learnt to work out the nutritional value and price cost of the meals. The best things I do well in, is presenting my work, I also enjoyed it. I've improved on presenting my work. To make things go even better on my next project, I will actually change the need of the people, and maybe the age-group. That way I'd be setting myself another challenge. I would probably present my work in a different style, but that all dephonds on my next brief.

WORKING WITH FOOD MATERIALS

LEVEL 5
THEME: SNACK FOODS
CONTEXT: BUSINESS & INDUSTRY
PROJECT: CRUNCHIE BAR
PUPIL: SUKI

Getting started

Aim

A product development activity. The pupils had some experience of business education to draw on concerning point of sale and presentation. Teaching was planned to cover appropriate food-processing methods for storing such products. The project's structure required pupils to look carefully at the potential market for their product and then to identify consumer preferences.

Assessment 1

Suki was able to identify the demand by young people for snackfoods before using her own preferences to suggest a chocolate-coated bar. She then recorded the results of her research into people's preferences before developing the product recipe.
(Evidence for Tes 1.5b, 2.5b, 2.5c, 4.5a.)

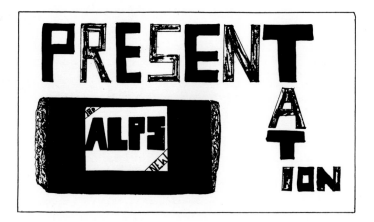

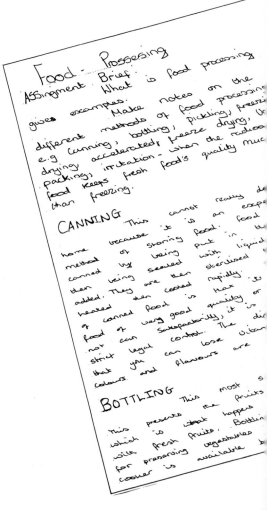

FREEZING

temperatures of the vegetables will not be high enough after storage to be safe.

Storing foods at low temperatures. This helps prevents their growth but does not stop it, so when taken out of freezing they will thaw and continue to grow. This prevents decaying freezer packing must be airtight and waterproof to retain flavour and prevent dehydration.

DRYING

This is a removal of moisture. This is very old method. Meat, fish, fruit etc were dried by the sun and the wind. In some countries it is still done this way but it is usually done commercially nowadays. Dried foods save storage space. They form a part of the convenience food. If moisture gets in it will enable organisms to grow, and they will decay.

ACCELERATED FREEZE DRYING

There are quick-frozen foods which have been marketed in great variety for the past few years, must be stored at low temperatures. Refrigeration is necessary during processing, transport and storage before the food reaches the consumer. This is a combination of both, freezing and drying but the processing method is new and has many advantages over

---

old methods. Food is prepared by ...wing unwanted parts - bone, gristle, fat, ..., etc.- and is immediately quick-frozen. ...s of the frozen food are placed in ...hamber from between -20°C and -30°C ...then heat is applied. After some hours ...water is reduced to as little as 2%. ...moisture in the food has been ...ved as vapour not as water. The ...ntages of freeze dried products are ...natural flavour and colouring is kept. ...claims to have all its nutrients, ...needs no special storage conditions ...it is simple preparations for cooking

...CKLING

This an old method. ...is were vegetables were pickled in ...gar and other acidy substances. In some ...tries this is still done, but it is ...very common way and is not ... ...effective method of preserving foods.

...uum PACKING

This when all the ...is taken out of the packet then ...d. An example of this is fruit juices. ...is vacuumed out by hot air. It prevents ...from decaying and bacteria.

...re
...so

...aits.
...aying
...le
...ecommend
...essure
...you dont

Brief: <u>New food Product Assignment</u>.
Design and develp a new food product for the food market

We had a group of three people and we decided between us about the food product we would develp. We all did different aspects of this project and put our results to together. Our first problem was what food we should do. Which part in the food market we should go into. So we decided on doing a pie chart showing what people eat most in a day.

WORKING WITH FOOD
MATERIALS

LEVEL 5
THEME: SNACK FOODS
CONTEXT: BUSINESS & INDUSTRY
PROJECT: CRUNCHIE BAR
PUPIL: SUKI

Developing ideas

Teacher's comments

Suki presented a fairly
coherent picture of her
work during the project.
Once she had the 'bar' idea
I taught her about methods
for making ingredients
stick together. Little was
recorded of her struggle in
getting the ingredients
right in terms of the
texture, density and
appearance of the bar. She
has recorded more on the
business aspects of her
proposal, but only in very
sketchy terms. I am
planning a mini-enterprise
project to focus on bulk
production and costings.

Assessment 2

The recipe for the bar was
put together after an
evaluation of existing
biscuit recipes. Suki
wanted the bar to have a
slightly chewier texture
than the biscuits in the
recipes she found. She has
recorded a few notes about
the changes she made to
the recipe.
*(Evidence for Tes 2.5b,
2.5c, 3.5a, 4.5b.)*

Alps Production.

We Decided on this Shape for our Alps bar. Also that the Slogan on the side of the bar Should be The CRAZY NUTY, CHEWIE, MUNCHY CRUNCHY CHOCOLATE BAR. The package we use will be able to be put in the fridge or freezer. The Size's will be Small, medium and large so their is a variety of prices and Sizes to buy. They will be samples put in Stores to see which of these Sizes are The most popular. Before we put the Alps bar on the market we would g posters and leaflets to introduce wrapper will be foil over the chocolate then a covering

---

Graph of
From the Su
product will b
-ide what age
at. We have
which age group
Schocolate. We
25-40 of they
bar. We also a
Senior citerfens
25.

100%

80%

60%

40%

20%

Young Adults A
(12-25)

Questionnaire for new Alps bar

Do you prefer sweet or Savory Biscuits?
We asked ten people this question. Seven out of ten said they prefer sweet biscuits.
Do you prefer your biscuits to be packaged in large numbers or in singular packages e.g chocolate bar?
We asked the same ten people, And nine out of ten said they prefered Singular packages.
What is the limit amount of money you would be prepared to pay for a chocolate bar?
We asked ten people. 15p-20p Seven people said this would be their limit. 20p-25p two people said this would be their limit. 25p-30p one person said this would be their limit.
Do you prefer biscuits made with white or wholemeal flour?
We asked ten people this question Seven said they prefered white flour and three said they prefered wholemeal flour.
Would you prefer a plain chocolate biscuit or a Milk chocolate biscuit.
We asked ten people. five said they prefered Milk and five said they prefered plain chocolate.
We are planning to put on the market a new type of snack bar called Alps priced 18p. It consists of oats chocolate chips and raisons and coated in chocolate. Would you be prepared to buy such a chocolate?
We asked ten people. Nine said yes they try it. One said No he doesn't like to try anything

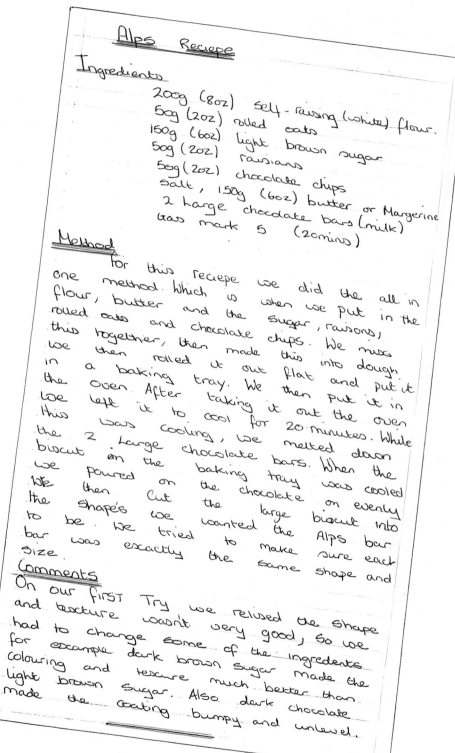

Alps Reciepe

Ingredients

200g (8oz) self-raising (white) flour.
50g (2oz) rolled oats
150g (6oz) light brown sugar
50g (2oz) raisians
50g (2oz) chocolate chips
salt, 150g (6oz) butter or Margerine
2 large chocolate bars (milk)
Gas mark 5 (20mins)

Method

For this reciepe we did the all in one method. Which is when we put in the flour, butter and the sugar, raisions, rolled oats and chocolate chips. We mix this together, then made this into dough. We then rolled it out flat and put it in a baking tray. We then put it in the oven. After taking it out the oven we left it to cool for 20 minutes. While this was cooling, we melted down the 2 large chocolate bars. When the biscut on the baking tray was cooled we poured on the chocolate on evenly. We then cut the large biscut into the shape's we wanted the Alps bar to be. We tried to make sure each bar was exactly the same shape and size.

Comments

On our first Try we relised the shape and texture wasn't very good, so we had to change some of the ingredents for example dark brown sugar made the colouring and texture much better than light brown sugar. Also dark chocolate made the coating bumpy and unlevel.

decided on the
Now we have to dec-
will aim our product
bar chart to Show
tly by a new bar of
en Adults age between
buy a new chocolate
Same Question to ten
Young Adults aged 12-

Seinor Citerens
(40 - 75)

WORKING WITH FOOD MATERIALS

LEVEL 5
THEME: SNACK FOODS
CONTEXT: & INDUSTRY
PROJECT: CRUNCHIE BAR
PUPIL: SUKI

Making things happen

Project review

How successful was the brief for pupils working at levels 4-7?
How would you have intervened to ensure that Suki recorded more of her thoughts and actions?
How important is it that Suki did not apply any of the information on food processing from the start of the project?
How would you have structured this activity so that pupils at higher levels were able effectively to take account of the business issues within the project?

Assessment 3

Suki has not managed to record how well her product met the needs of its potential customers. This makes the assessment of Te4 quite limited. However, she does review her thinking and actions throughout her work, as well as evaluate data from her research and use this in a constructive way.
(Evidence for Tes 2.5b, 2.5c, 2.5d, 3.5a, 3.5b, 3.5d, 4.5a, 4.5b.)

Production Alps Report
Our product is a type of crunch...
coated in plain or milk chocolate...
of just having an ordinary biscui...
thought of adding raisins, chocola...
and oats to give it a crunch...
When we made the biscuit the...
and texture did not turn out...
would have anticipated. To impr...
shape we would have to...
of mould 4 it was to be m...
The name we chose is Alps...
wrapping would be similar to...
Twix or Mars bar. Each packe...
consist of two biscuits and...
have a starting price of 18p...
out market research we fou...
majority of people that we...
Questionaire at, said they'd...
biscuit to be made with...
flour rather than wholemea...
also found that given a...
and milk chocolate, peop...
milk the most Our prod...
at all ends of the...
youngsters to teenagers a...
to promote the new p...

could also give away free mini. Samples of the product, issue posters to be put up on bill boards and Shop windows. These are cheap ways. A more expensive way to promote the Alps bar would be to advertise on t.v and on Radio's.
The point of Sale would be newsagents, Off licences, Corner Shops and at cash desks in large well known stores for example Sainsburys or Tescos

Conclusion

We chose to do an Alps bar because - as you can see in our reserch - chocolate is what is in demand on the food market today. We also think that we could make a better chocolate which will be enjoyed and be in popular demand like crunchy or mars bars. I enjoyed this product but I didn't realise how much reserch was involved. It was intresting to find out what people mainly eat through the day and how not alot of people have three main meals a day but snacks or through the day. Research was fun and interesting to do and I enjoyed the whole project alot. Maybe we could have done a bit more Reserch also we could have presented it better, but on the whole I think we did okay.

WORKING WITH FOOD MATERIALS

LEVEL 6
THEME: SNACK FOODS
CONTEXT: BUSINESS & INDUSTRY
PROJECT: VEGETARIAN BURGER
PUPIL: PRITAM

Getting started

Aim

To develop realistic recipe ideas for a new 'takeaway' fast food. The emphasis was on pupils using trials to assess different recipe ideas. Pupils built on exploratory work that they had done in mapping out methods of combining similar ingredients to achieve different end results. Pupils were also expected to use nutritional analysis to judge the combinations they were developing. They were also asked to report in detail on the success of their methods and results for a chosen consumer group. Pupils worked in pairs but were expected to write up their work individually.

Assessment 1

Pritam seems to have gone into the project with a clear view of what is available in fast-food outlets, so her thinking was based on experience rather than actual research. There is little real evidence to justify her conclusions. (This omission may have contributed to the way she evaluated her working.) *(Evidence of Tes 1.6a, 2.6c.)*

Brief

You have been asked to develop and try out a range of fast-food dishes for a local fast-food restaurant.

All the dishes you make must be
a) Quick, easy and economical to prepare
b) Popular with the customers

c) Nutritious

Identifying The Problem

First of all we needed to find out exactly what was meant by the word nutritious. From information in books we found that nutrition is the study of the chemical composition of foods and how the body uses food. All food is made up of chemical substances known as nutrients. These are absorbed and used by the body to keep us alive. Water may also be considered as a nutrient, since it is vital for life. The nutrients are proteins, fats, carbohydrates, vitamins and minerals.

these nutrients cannot
and in just one food,
fferent foods need
e eaten to have a
amount. Nutrients
needed in varying
ts depending on the
and sex of a person.

STAGE 1
first decided that there
o need for starters
serts because people
dont
ly havant them from
ood chains. People tend
ally buy burgers from
ood restaurants, so we
t that we would have
as well. But healthier
. such as
N BURGERS, KIDNEY BEAN
AND CHICK PEA BURGERS.
e side order we thought of
with a dip as this
extra fat in it.
lso decided to make
made from fresh fruit
m.

I thought that it was important to think about how fast food could be made more nutritious, but still be fast to prepare and cook and be ready quickly to order for the customer because lots of people eat a large amount of fast foods and from what I have seen when I have been eating out, they are often made from cheap, rubbishy foods.

Beef Burger Recipe

Ingredients
8ozs minced beef
1 chopped onion
3 peeled and chopped tomatoes
2 tps mixed herbs
black pepper
1 egg optional

Once we had decided on burgers, our starting point was to look at existing burger recipes in school recipe books and some at home. The most standard recipe we found was the one we took as our base for further developing.

WORKING WITH FOOD MATERIALS

LEVEL 6
THEME: SNACK FOODS
CONTEXT: BUSINESS & INDUSTRY
PROJECT: VEGETARIAN BURGER
PUPIL: PRITAM

Developing ideas

Teacher 's comments

I was concerned about being able to assess the individual contributions of Pritam and her partner, so during the activity I tried to see the pair several times, to question each on their thinking and decision taking. I used this observational evidence to check the validity of each pupil's project report. Pritam has reported fairly on her working and I feel that her conclusions show a clear understanding of her objectives and ideas during the project. However, she did not identify clearly enough a user group and this means that her evaluation is too general.

Assessment 2

Again it would seem that a lack of initial thinking and research has lead to little in the way of a specification or objectives for recipe developement. However there is considerable evidence of the knowledge and understanding about the materials that Pritam used in working out how to convert the beef recipe for vegetarians using beans.
(Evidence of Tes 2.6b, 2.6c, 3.6a, 3.6b, 3.6c, 3.6d.)

STAGE 2
We chose to cook the soya burger, kidney burger; the dip and the drinks

SOYABURGER
Ingredients - 1 chopped onion
3 peeled tomatoes
Black pepper
½ cup wholewheat breadcrumbs
3 cups cooked soya beans
2 tsps mixed herbs
1 egg (optional)

Quick, easy and economical-
The soya burgers do need a lot of preparation time so we think it is better to make them and freeze them so that when you want to eat them you just fry them or grill them.

Nutritious-
Soya beans are a good substitute for meat. They are a good source of protein. The burgers are also suitable for vegetarians

Ingred

QUICK
nee
cook
we
eng
the
Nutri
a
cook
carb

DIP
Ingredients - cucumber
Tomatoes
Salad cream

Quick, Easy, Economical
This was very qu
we just blended the cuc
tomatoes and added
Nutritious- Salad cream was
and too high in fat. A
we could substitute th
cream with sour crea
yoghurt which wour
lower in fat and high

ANBURGER
n of red kidney beans
nion
peeled tomatoes
cups fresh breadcrumbs
asoning

Economical -
Kidney bean burgers
same type of
the soya burgers, but
these ones up fresh.
se to grill them, brush-
with oil to reduce
nt of fat in them.

e did have less fat
the difference in
se are also high in
es.

How we developed the burgers
We had done some previous work on pulses (beans) and what they
could be used for, so we knew that beans were a good
substitute for meat. This is because:
(a) nutritionally they are similar
(b) they can be mashed and mixed to behave as a binder for
    other ingredients
(c) they are inexpensive.

Quite a lot of recipes in wholefood and vegetarian books use
beans (especially kidney beans because of the red colour)
instead of meat, so it must be an idea which had been tried
and tested. We wanted to use beans which, when cooked and
mashed, are waxy in texture rather than lentils which can be
wetter, because we thought that they would help to bind the
mixture better. Also, we carried out some market research in
and around our local area and asked people who ran the fast
food outlets to tell us what their most popular lines were at
the moment.

For this assignment we will concentrate mainly on the burgers
because these provide a very interesting challenge and will
probably take the most time to develop from scratch.

We carried out an experiment with lentils, soya beans and
kidney beans. We took a small amount of each (cooked) and
mixed them with egg. The same amount in each case so that it
would be a fair test. We looked at the result and then added
breadcrumbs to each. We decided that the breadcrumbs were
helpful in binding the mixture together. They helped to
absorb the egg and gave the mixture bulk and structure.

We know from other work that some ingredients are useful for
binding ingredients together - like eggs, oatmeal,
breadcrumbs, flour - when mixed with liquid they become gluey
and then set when cooked to give firmness.

nake.
and
cream.
protein
lternative
y
natural
much
protein

PEACHES/STRAWBERRIES AND
CREAM DRINK

Quick, Easy, Economical - We simply blended
each fruit with 1 carton of cream.

Nutritious - We used single cream as
this had the least amount of fat
in it. But we could have used
something with a lower fat content
for example skimmed milk.

WORKING WITH FOOD MATERIALS

LEVEL 6
THEME: SNACK FOODS
CONTEXT: BUSINESS & INDUSTRY
PROJECT: VEGETARIAN BURGER
PUPIL: PRITAM

Making things happen

Project review

Would you have allowed Pritam (and her partner) to focus on as many as three or four dishes?

What are the best ways of enabling pupils to trial their food prototypes without undue wastage?

When would you have intervened to ensure that Pritam took account of the needs of her product's potential consumers?

How can you help pupils to develop work in materials without loosing sight of the design context?

How would you intervene to ensure that pupils plan their projects so that there is enough time for testing and evaluation after making?

How effective was this project as a piece of product-development work?

Assessment 3

Pritam has recorded the problems and results for each of the recipes she developed, and gave a chart for ease of comparison. It is clear from her final evaluation that she is aware that there were aspects of the context that she had not taken into account which resulted in a comparatively subjective appraisal of her work. This realization needs to be built on in future work. *(Evidence of Tes 3.6a, 3.6b, 3.6c, 3.6d, 3.6e, 4.6a, 4.6b, 4.6c, 4.6d.)*

Results

We both thought that both the burgers turned out well with wholemeal rolls without any butter or margarine. A low fat chutney, relish or spread could be spread over the rolls to make them moist.

However the dip became a little to runny as we put too much salad cream in it.

Both of the drinks were quite thick and still had too much fat in them. We found that they tasted much

From doing this assignment I learned to do a lot of new things.

I found out what nutritious actually meant as opposed to what I the it had meant.

We had to plan our time ahead to do practi as we were soon to sta work experience. ie. time had to be organised efficiently

However we did ac our aims despite the time we had.

I learnt more abou the nutritional content of foods and how to make which I had never m before.

Finding A Fast Food Product	Developing The Recipe	Ease of making/ Quicker method	Result of Recipe	Evaluation of Recipe
SOYA BEAN BURGER - healthier type of burger. also suitable for vegetarians.	3 cups Soya Beans (cooked) 1 Medium Sized onion Chillies optional Ginger optional 3 Tomatoes (peeled) 2 tecs Seasoning 1/4 tecs Salt + Pepper Pepper optional 1 Egg 1/2 cup wholewheat	The Burger should be easier to make using a food processor for chopping and blending etc. The burger mixture can be put into a burger maker and then finally grilled 10-12 mins medium heat.	The result was a tasty burger. It was a little too dry especially with a bun. So an alternative to ketchup should cut down the dryness.	If someone would like to have the burger alone then it can be coated in oil to soften it up.
KIDNEY BEAN BURGER - healthier type of burger and also suitable vegetarians.	one tin of kidney beans one medium sliced onion Breadcrumbs to cover the burger Salt + Pepper			when you put the burger in the bun margarine would be better and also healthier if it was a wholemeal bun.
CHICK PEA BURGER - which type of burger but still as nutritious	Same ingredients as the kidney bean burger but using a tin of chick-peas instead		This burger was much drier than the rest and still tasted dry when fried	We decided we already had enough burgers so we scraped this one as it was the driest out of them all
DIP + TOMATO + CUCUMBER - a is to be used as ketchup is on burgers.	30g Salad Cream 1kg Cucumber 5cm 1 tomato	The cucumber is to be shredded and so is the tomato. This can be done in the food processor. Then the salad cream can be poured in slowly	The dip was nice. It did mosten the burger and gave it a tangy sort of taste.	A little less salad cream should be used as it was a little runny. This dip can be used inside the burger.
STRAWBERRY AND MELON DRINK - A drink made out of fruits only.	One box of strawberries Half a melon	The ingredients can be blended in a food processor or with a hand blender	The drink looked disgusting and would put people off. It also had a furry taste A Horrible flavour	we didn't like the idea of the drink so well try another one. instead try another one.
STRAWBERRY + CREAM DRINK - Strawberries and milk make a fresh milk shake	One glass of milk One scoop low fat vanilla icecream 3-4 strawberries	After putting the icecream into the milk slice each strawberry into four place it on top.	The drink was beautiful. It looked nice and tasted delicious.	The drink was very nice and is ideal for the summer.
PEACHES + CREAM DRINK Peaches instead of strawberries for a different flavour.	Same ingredients except using one sliced peach			
SALAD - A vegetable salad fruit salad.	Variety of vegetables or variety of fruits	slicing or chopping can be done in a food processor	Both recipe were nice and tasty.	For extra taste fresh cream can be used on the fruit salad.

WORKING WITH RESISTANT MATERIALS

LEVEL 3
THEME: ON THE MOVE
CONTEXT: COMMUNITY
PROJECT: CAN CRUSHER
PUPIL: JIM

Getting started

Aim

To encourage pupils to work constructively together. Based on 'taking your home with you', it looked at living on the move. Each class was split into mixed ability groups which had to identify an aspect of the topic to work on (e.g. shelter, food, storage, entertainment). As the topic was potentially so diverse the groups started in a base room but then negotiated to work in an appropriate specialist area, once their idea developed clarity. Teachers acted as experts giving support and advice *or* teaching as necessary.

Assessment 1

Jim and his partner were able to discuss their thoughts and ideas to come up with a real need. They worked from direct experience of crushing cans to thinking about the ways this task could be managed. *(Evidence of Tes 1.3a, 1.3b.)*

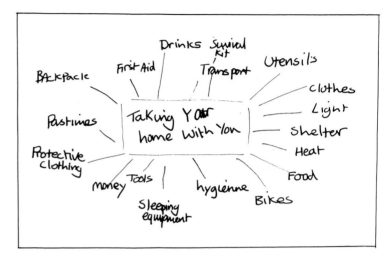

Our project 'taking your home with you'. We looked at a tent, cooking utensils a coach and ~~cooking~~ looking at books We recorded our information on ~~the~~ working sheet 1.
     On the coach we were shown the toilets the entertainment t.V. etc.. The tent was a two/three man tent. When it was taken down it was compact. One of the problems was litter, our group have decided to ~~md~~ design and make a 'can crusher'
Some of the problems we will have to overcome

The most usefull information was the other people in the class discusing the problems of rubbish disposiel in a remoate place. I think he trip onto the coach was not very helpfull because the eacher talked about the video and t.v. and we could proberly never awe enaugh time (12brs) to design and make a new ~~video~~ t.v in the short space of time.

he way we are deciding which is our best idea is o debate with the rest of the group the pros and cons of the dea the time also plays a major part. Brainstorming was a ood idea because it gave us scope to find more ideas and make our first ones better. Our final ideal is a can crusher.

he main problems we ~~totittle~~ will have will proberbly be he crusher hinge, and making the pressure big enough to crush the can. ~~tha~~ we could use books and look at ~~thinte~~ hings with hinges eg doors, car doors, cupboards etc . . . t find strong materials

5 make our project sucsesfull we will have to make the an crusher compact, light and easy to use. Like i wrote in Planning and making we could use other hinges ideas.

WORKING WITH RESISTANT MATERIALS

LEVEL 3
THEME: ON THE MOVE
CONTEXT: COMMUNITY
PROJECT: CAN CRUSHER
PUPIL: JIM

Developing ideas

Teacher's comments

Jim collaborated very successfully with a partner here. Working together provided sufficient stimulus for both pupils to make and test their can crusher. In previous projects both pupils ran out of steam! Their discussions enabled a real need to be identified and, with some prompting, Jim showed how they considered simple mechanisms for squashing or even mincing their cans. It is clear from discussion that they realized that a holding device was a sensible starting point, with the force provided by stamping on the gadget. There is almost no evidence for this idea.

Assessment 2

Jim and his partner worked initially on a folding crusher, but could not solve the problem of a 'strong-enough hinge'. Little is recorded of this. After consultation they came up with the idea of a simple base block to support the can, with an upper block which would give a uniform 'crush', and springs for easy ejection of the crushed can.
(Evidence of Tes 2.3a, 2.3d, 2.3e, 3.3d.)

The new information we needed was what material to use for the main Body of the crusher without it being to heavy. Time badly effected our design because now we get to make we have only got two weeks left! Which means the design has to be si and easy to make.

we got our ideas from each other and got help on the material from our schools C.DT Department. We also need to Know how the materials are.

Our ideas which were rejected were through trial and error by draw the idea into the design and asking various people.

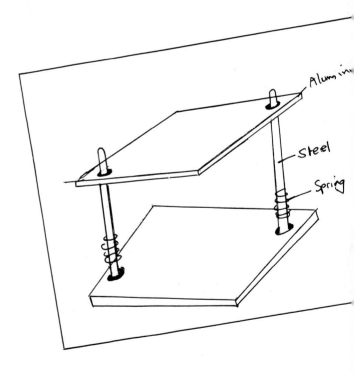

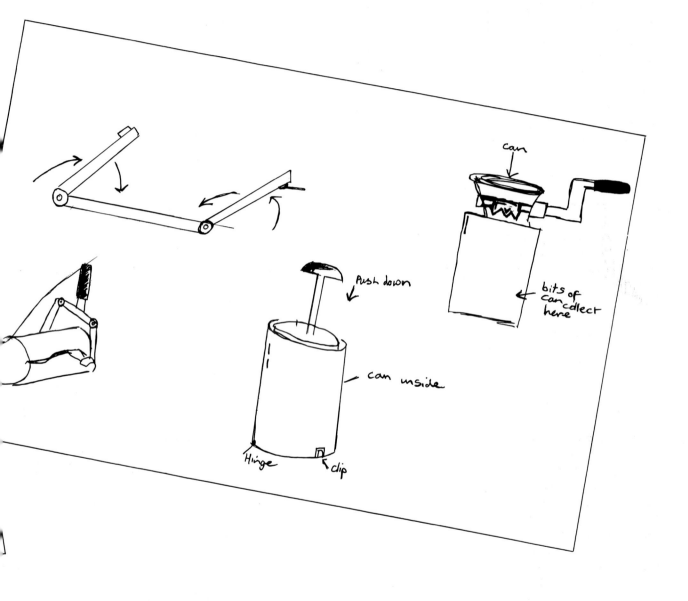

can

Push down

Can inside

bits of
can collect
here

Hinge

clip

WORKING WITH RESISTANT MATERIALS

LEVEL 3
THEME: ON THE MOVE
CONTEXT: COMMUNITY
PROJECT: CAN CRUSHER
PUPIL: JIM

Making things happen

Project review

How could Jim's project idea be elaborated as a teaching vehicle for work on simple mechanisms and testing?
How could Jim have been encouraged to develop his capability and demonstrate the knowledge underpinning his ideas?
What ways can you think of for assessing paired or group projects?
How could pupils be encouraged to record their individual ideas and actions when they are working with others?
How could the project's structure, of groups working on different aspects of a topic, be linked to allow the ideas to be seen and evaluated as part of a whole?

Assessment 3

They had considerable problems in getting their idea to work; hinges, split wood, etc. The pair worked by trial and error, without really having any ideas of ways of using force to an advantage. Jim's evaluation is based on design considerations - light and compact, not heavy and cumbersome, working effectiveness - as well as production difficulties.
(Evidence of Tes 2.3d, 3.3a, 3.3b, 3.3d, 4.3a, 4.3b.)

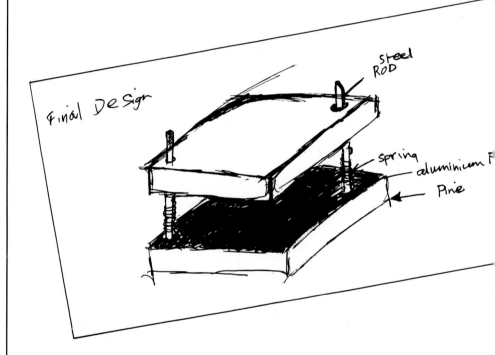

Final Design
steel ROD
spring
aluminium P
Pine

We found that our prototype design was too heavy an
so we refined it to our present design which is light
which is slightly more effective.

t first we missed out on our 'can crusher' being compact and light as soon as we reilesed our mistake we amended our design to our requirements.

We developed our ideas to close a gap in peoples needs. We think we used enough information but did not have the time to devlop it!

We did not plan for the wood to split but when it happened we changed our ideas. We improved our ideas in we made it lighter and more compacted

Our solution work to a certain degree although the time did effect it. We did not have much help but we still used our own ideas

some

e compact

WORKING WITH RESISTANT MATERIALS

LEVEL 4
THEME: WEATHER
CONTEXT: COMMUNITY
PROJECT: WARNING INDICATOR
PUPIL: TOM

Getting started

Aim

To look at ways of using new technologies in meeting people's needs. An informal evaluation of electronic sensors and their uses was introduced and information provided on circuits. Pupils had some experience of making electronic circuits, but this was their first opportunity to design an artefact or system. Some teaching was given on input/control/output thinking as a way of developing appropriate devices.

Assessment 1

The group's discussion of adverse weather and Tom's own thinking led him to identify a real need for a flood-warning device. Little mention is made of how such a device will be used or of user needs. Some early ideas about how to achieve a warning using a device that moves with rising water.
(Evidence of Tes 1.4a, 1.4d, 1.4e, 2.4a, 2.4b.)

You have had a short introduction to the theme of weather we would like you to try to focus on a need related to weather in the context of the home, especially thinking about the needs of the elderly and the young.

I think their is a need for :
A high-tide indicator because many rivers flood when there is a high tide. Many nearby houses get flooded.

The aim of my design proposal is to :
1. build a high tide indicator which will send out a signal.

2.

3.

You will have to find out some information for yourself, during the next week to make sure that your proposals are realistic, in this last section you have to list where you are going to find out the information, how you are going to collect it and devise a method of presenting it.

I intend to find out more about my possible ideas using the following methods of research.

My design is aimed at homes which are near rivers, I decided on this because many rivers flood during heavy rain. This causes widespread destruction throughout the house. My design is going to be a river level indicator. If the water rises past a certain level an alarm will sound. Occupants of homes would be able to move furniture to a higher level.

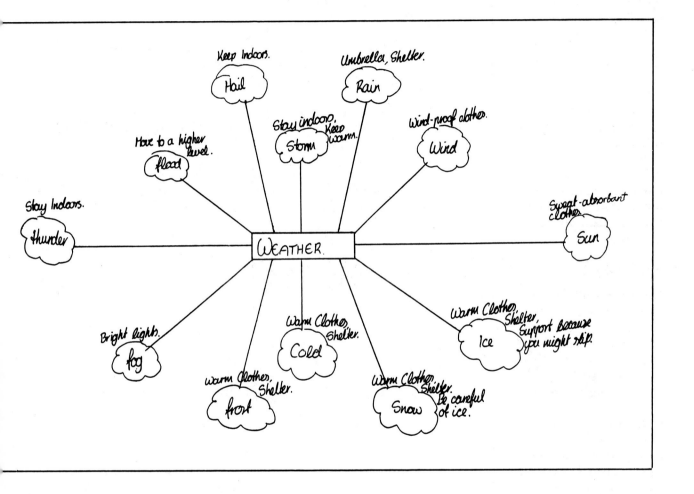

WORKING WITH RESISTANT MATERIALS

LEVEL 4
THEME: WEATHER
CONTEXT: COMMUNITY
PROJECT: WARNING INDICATOR
PUPIL: TOM

Developing ideas

Teacher's comments

Tom had a good initial idea and had sufficient experience to develop this into a workable proposition. His final idea was based on a mechanical rather than an electronic solution, which seemed appropriate. He needed advice about producing his idea within the time constraints. This involved using ready-made piping to reduce the making time. I was disappointed that he did not manage to test his idea and so produced sketchy final evaluation.

Assessment 2

Tom shows that his overriding concern is getting his idea made and working. He uses graphic techniques to communicate effectively how his idea is meant to work. He also recorded some of the decisions he has to make about selecting appropriate materials and establishing the need for new knowledge and understanding.
(Evidence of Tes 1.4b, 2.4a, 2.4b, 2.4c, 3.4c.)

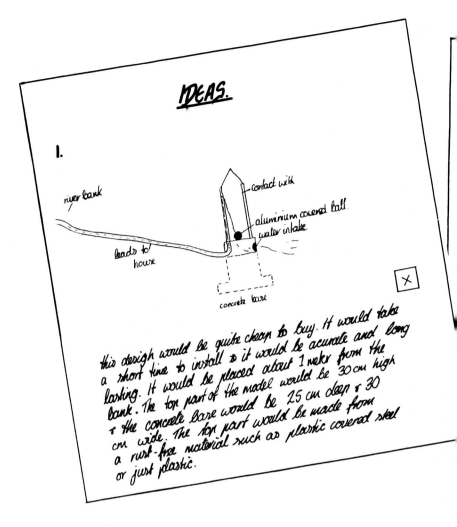

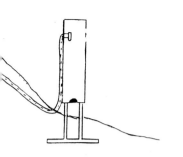

nd design uses a moisture sensor.
be placed in a small box to protect
he rain which might set it off.
I also have a small baffler in front
that waves wouldn't touch the sensor.

✓

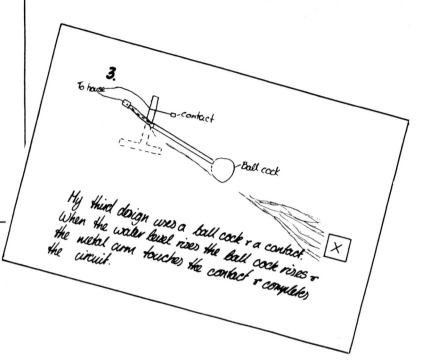

My third design uses a ball cock & a contact.
When the water level rises the ball cock rises &
the metal arm touches the contact & completes
the circuit.

✗

I researched the aspect of all types of weather :- sun, rain, wind, snow, flood! I came up with the idea that flood
causes most destruction. I also decided on my brief - a flood warning, because my grandparents live by a river in
Yorkshire & it often got flooded. In fact, the building had to be rebuilt because of the damage done.
    I have come up with 3 ideas, one using a moisture sensor, one using a ball cock mechanism & one using
a contact wire mechanism. I do not really know which design to use.

I have had 3 ideas. Each will have to be cheap to buy & run & will have to last a long time.
The first one uses a moisture sensor in a box. This will send out a signal when water makes a contact. It is protected
by waves by a baffler. The second uses a ballcock mechanism rather like ones found in toilets. This wouldn't be
very good because of waves. The third is a ball rising in a box with the river level. When the ball gets to a
certain height it touches some wires & makes a contact! We have all done this thing at school.

I would use treated wood or steel for all designs. This is because they would need to last a long time.
In one design I need a concrete base. This would be difficult to make & it might deteriorate under water.
In all designs wires lead to a control box which is in the house. The easiest one to do & build will be the
moisture sensor one.

I have got 15 hours to build it. My design needs to be accurate as well as cheap to make.
I need to look at materials in which to build it with. I need to look at present designs for water level makes & I
might design a protector for doors to keep the water out.

WORKING WITH RESISTANT MATERIALS

LEVEL 4
THEME: WEATHER
CONTEXT: COMMUNITY
PROJECT: WARNING INDICATOR
PUPIL: TOM

Making things happen

Project review

How could Tom have been encouraged to record more of his thinking, ideas and working?

What evidence is there that Tom was clear about the function and use of his design?

How appropriate is it for pupils to use 'ready-made' or 'bought-in' components in realizing their design ideas?

How should projects requiring design based on high levels of technical understanding be structured to achieve an appropriate balance of learning and design-based application?

Assessment 3

During the project Tom made decisions based on a good understanding of what his device needed to be like (water resistant and durable). He changed and modified his ideas as they progressed. Tom was obviously extremely pleased to have produced his device, given the time constraints. His final evaluation is limited as it focuses on how he made the device, rather than how effective or appropriate it was.
(Evidence of Tes 3.4a, 3.4b, 3.4d, 3.4e, 4.4a 4.4b.)

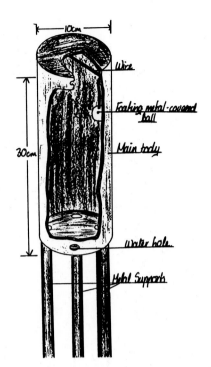

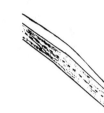

Use the list below to order your material, if you require wood, metal or plastics you must give three dimensions along with the number you need and what part the material will eventually make e.g. side. Textiles should be ordered in a similar manner except it may not be necessary to give the thickness of the material. If you require food then you must list the ingredients along with the quantity e.g. 10 grammes.

MATERIAL/ TEXTILE	LENGTH	WIDTH	THICKNESS	PART	NO. REQD.	COMMENT
					1	Main Body
Down pipe	300	100	100		4	Supports.
Copper pipe	800	25	25		1	Ping Pong ball.
Plastic ball.	40	40	40			
Wire.	4000	—			1	
Buzzer.					2	Top + Bottom
Perspex.	120	120			1.	9 volt.
Battery.						
INGREDIENTS				QUANTITY		

Air Hole

Connection Wire.

...ion wire

Aluminium (metal)
...covered floatable
ball.

Water Hole   Supports.

1. Over the last few months or weeks I have learnt many things.
First of all I have learnt how to design something within
someones ability to make the thing in 5 lessons. I have learnt
how to use perspex + the glue gun + during lessons I have
been able to look at other peoples work + learn some skills
that they have used

2. I think that I did most of the things well. I did a
clear picture explaining my idea + I got my equipment
+ made the thing well. The only thing I didn't do
well was not looking around for materials + looking for
cheaper stuff

3. On my next project I will try to do something that
really test me. I will try to work quicker + get the necessary
equipment in so that I will finish with a good product.

LIST OF ITEMS NEEDED FOR WATER INDICATOR.

1. Stainless Steel or plastic piping (30 x 10cm.)
2. 3 copper piping supports. (3 x 100cm)
3. 1 Aluminium - foil covered ping-pong ball.
4. Plastic - covered copper wiring.
5. 1.5 volt battery.
6. 1 buzzer.
7. Stainless Steel or plastic top + bottom for main body (10 x 10)

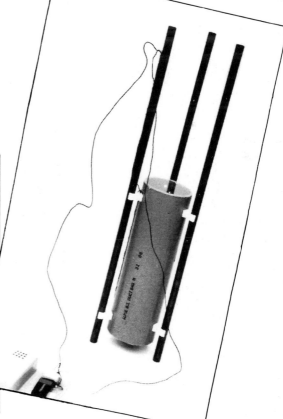

...oked moving at the type of equipment I would use.
...my main body because it doesn't rust + it is quite cheap.
...in this way + with this in mind it was easy to work with.
...research for my idea because I had already made up my idea.
...research I am sure that I would have got the wrong equipment.

...as as I did because I had in my mind a cheap, maintenance free
...to build because I only had 5 lessons in which to build it.
...I would probably take the item home + paint it so that it would
...had to come in at lunch times to do some work but I think that
...I feel that I put in a lot of thought + effort while doing it my

...eneficial to my end result. My planning was good because I knew how I would
...of my thing. I thought that I made my thing well + it worked first time
...wouldn't plan differently but I would make it a bit quicker, maybe making

...that I have worked quite well + I am pleased with my result
...body + the legs don't move but the box with the buzzer in could
...being glued because changing the battery will be quite hard
...enjoyed this project + I am very pleased with the result.

WORKING WITH RESISTANT MATERIALS

LEVEL 5
THEME: WEATHER
CONTEXT: SCHOOL
PROJECT: EDUCATIONAL AID
PUPIL: PAUL

Getting started

Aim

This group had considerable experience of design-based projects but not for a targeted user group. So this topic was set up to encourage pupils to research into and take account of primary children's needs in learning about the weather. Experience from assessing previous projects showed how rarely pupils recorded their ideas and decisions about production issues and processes. So pupils were asked to try and record as much of their thinking and decision making as possible, especially about making their artefact.

Assessment 1

Paul has three interesting ideas for teaching about weather, but given the time limit judged it best to develop the teaching thermometer. He raises several issues about how to make his idea interesting and workable, but does not sufficiently research into children's needs to achieve level 5 (see Te1.5a).
(Evidence of Tes 1.4a, 1.4d, 1.4e, 1.5b, 2.5a, 2.5e.)

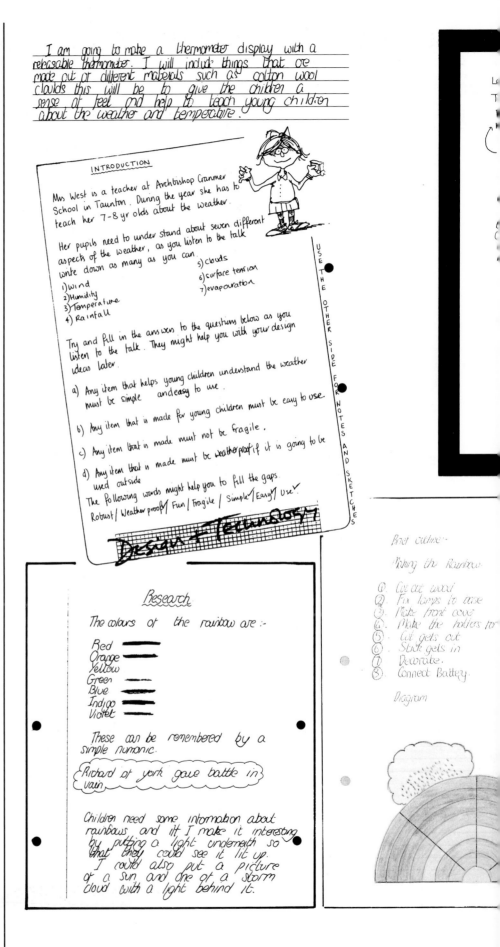

I am going to make a thermometer display with a releasable thermometer. I will include things that are made out of different materials such as cotton wool clouds this will be to give the children a sense of feel and help to teach young children about the weather and temperature.

INTRODUCTION

Mrs West is a teacher at Archbishop Cranmer School in Taunton. During the year she has to teach her 7-8 yr olds about the weather.

Her pupils need to understand about seven different aspects of the weather, as you listen to the talk write down as many as you can.
1) wind
2) Humidity
3) Temperature
4) Rainfall
5) clouds
6) surface tension
7) evapouration

USE THE OTHER SIDE FOR NOTES AND SKETCHES

Try and fill in the answers to the questions below as you listen to the talk. They might help you with your design ideas later.

a) Any item that helps young children understand the weather must be simple and easy to use.

b) Any item that is made for young children must be easy to use.

c) Any item that is made must not be fragile.

d) Any item that is made must be weatherproof if it is going to be used outside.
The following words might help you to fill the gaps.
Robust / Weatherproof / Fun / Fragile / Simple / Easy / Use

Design + Technology

Research

The colours of the rainbow are:-
Red
Orange
Yellow
Green
Blue
Indigo
Violet

These can be remembered by a simple numonic.

Richard of york gave battle in vain

Children need some information about rainbows and if I make it interesting by putting a light underneath so that they could see it lit up. I could also put a picture of a sun and one of a storm cloud with a light behind it.

First outline:-
Making the Rainbow
1. Cut out wood
2. Fix lamps to case
3. Make front cover
4. Make the holders for
5. Cut gels out
6. Stick gels in
7. Decorate
8. Connect Battery

Diagram

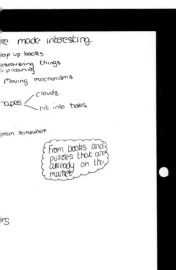

...re made interesting.

...op up books

...scovering things
...picturing

...Moving mechanisms

...apes ─ clouds.
        └ fit into holes

...from somewhere

From books and
puzzles that are
currently on the
market

...s

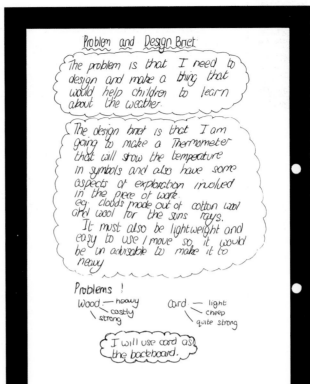

Problem and Design Brief

The problem is that I need to design and make a thing that would help children to learn about the weather.

The design brief is that I am going to make a Thermometer that will show the temperature in symbols and also have some aspects of exploration involved in the piece of work.
eg. clouds made out of cotton wool and wool for the suns rays.
It must also be lightweight and easy to use / move so it would be un advisable to make it to heavy

Problems !

Wood ── heavy
     ── costly
     └ strong

Card ── light
     ── cheep
     └ quite strong

I will use card as the backboard.

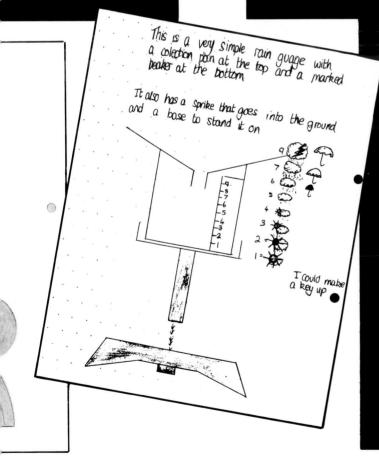

This is a very simple rain guage with a collection pan at the top and a marked beaker at the bottom

It also has a sprike that goes into the ground and a base to stand it on

9
8
7
6
5
4
3
2
1

I could make a key up ●

What is it all about :- Our project is about designing and making a piece of work that will help children to learn about the weather.

Who for :- They are for 7-8 year old primary school children.
To do what :- To make learning about the weather more exciting for them.

Why - Because at the moment it is hard for them to understand what the weather is about.

Like what - I am going to make a thermometer out of card and a science thermometer and different materials with different feels (texture). I also need to draw out my ideas for the design.

Finding things out - I also need to find things out from books about thermometers.

Can I do this - In the time I have I can do this

What I will need. Card   Thermometer   Glue
                  Cottonwool Wool Fabric Colours
                  Wood   Scissors

How long have I got. 5 weeks 12 hours
Making it successful. I will have to make it so that it looks good and professional.

What next. Then I need to evaluate my work and see if it can improved

Why I chose this.

I was going to make a rainbow that would light up but I do not think I have enough time to make this
   I then decided to make a thermometer with little pictures that would give young children and idea about heat and temperature linking up the two areas. If the clouds and sun are made out of different materials then it will give the children some-thing to touch.

WORKING WITH RESISTANT MATERIALS

LEVEL 5
THEME: WEATHER
CONTEXT: SCHOOL
PROJECT: EDUCATIONAL AID
PUPIL: PAUL

Developing ideas

Teacher's comments

Paul is a particularly reflective pupil, with sufficient capability to visualize and predict the details of his ideas (in a made form) allowing him to come up with realistic and considered plans for making. His idea for the teaching aspect of his project was to enable young children to make the link between temperature and likely weather, through visual images surrounding a thermometer. This meant that much of his work was concerned with achieving sufficient quality in the visual and textural treatment of symbols. He also considered, in some detail, how the thermometer would be used, mounted and made accessible.

Assessment 2

Paul produced a considerable range of evidence describing what he did to detail his design and plan realistically for its production. He justifies most of his decisions using his knowledge of working with materials ('yellow sticky paper when mixed with paint gives a good effect for the sun'). *(Evidence of Tes 1.4c, 2.5a, 2.5b, 2.5e, 3.5a, 3.5d.)*

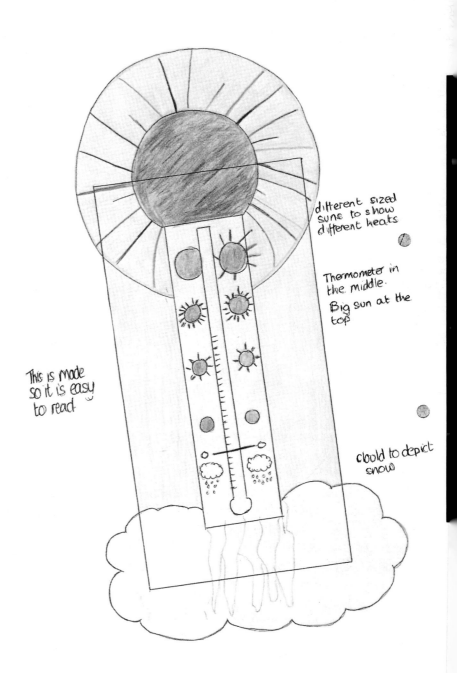

Before our 1st lesson I had many Ideas on different po was a very complicated and involved light circuits and s different spots that involved the colours of the rainba not a good idea as it would take alot of time to ~~tra~~ enough for the bulbs and batteries to be safe. Safety is hate to be overcome. My second idea was a rain guage for the time limit I had. The third and best idea was c

different sized suns to show different heats

Thermometer in the middle. Big sun at the top

This is made so it is easy to read

cloud to depict snow

...e weather. My first idea
...ferent coloured gels into the
...tter, alot of thought was
...ntainer and make it strong
...another problem, that would
...is too was too complicated
...meter with diagrams to show

...different types of weather.
...his also offered explanation for
...children with touch and the
...of being part of something.
...also must be easy to use
...children and I think that
...idea is.

...ard.
...backboard 160mm x 300mm.
...meter backboard 3.5mm x 210mm.
...sun = 55mm in diameter
...diameter including rays is 140mm
...on wool for clouds
...ite cord for cave entrance.
...stic to waterproof the thermometer

...Materials
...piece of card 300mm x 160mm
...ch poster card)
..., yellow, orange, red paints
...sky and for sun
...on wool.
...clouds.
...our other items such
...thin card and paper.

What to use.
I will use the materials available
and try and make it in a cost
effective way.
Coping with Problems
If I have problems that I cannot
overcome I will either ask people in
my classe who are doing more or
less the same thing or ask advice
from my Teacher
What do I need to decide.
I need to decide how I can use
my past experience in DT to make
my project successful.
Will it be suitable.
I have asked a few people and
they all say that this idea of
mine would be a good Idea.
Getting it to work out.
This links in with making it
successful and I need to look
at my results to get it to work out

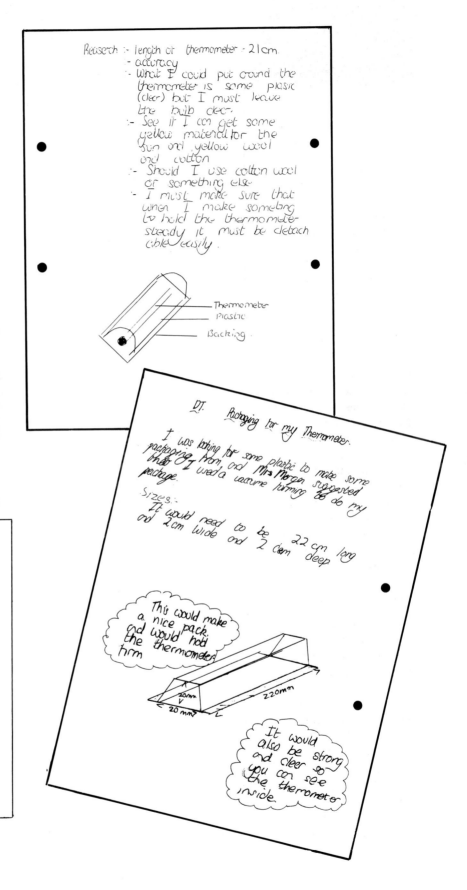

Reaserch :- length of thermometer - 21cm.
- accuracy
- What I could put around the
  thermometer is some plastic
  (clear) but I must leave
  the bulb clear.
- See if I can get some
  yellow material for the
  sun and yellow wool
  and cotton
- Should I use cotton wool
  or something else
- I must make sure that
  when I make something
  to hold the thermometer
  steady it must be detach
  -able easily.

Thermometer
Plastic
Backing.

DT. Packaging for my Thermometer.

I was looking for some plastic to make some
packaging from and Mrs Morgan suggested
that I used a vacuume forming to do my
package.

Sizes:
It would need to be 22 cm long
and 2 cm wide and 2 cm deep

This would make
a nice pack.
and would hold
the thermometer.
firm

10mm
220mm
20 mm

It would
also be strong
and clear so
you can see
the thermometer
inside.

WORKING WITH RESISTANT MATERIALS

LEVEL 5
THEME: WEATHER
CONTEXT: SCHOOL
PROJECT: EDUCATIONAL AID
PUPIL: PAUL

Making things happen

Project review

What techniques for researching into children's needs and visual imagery could have been used to help Paul broaden the scope of his ideas?
What aspects of knowledge and understanding were used during this project?
Would you have intervened to ensure that Paul used a wider range of materials?
Looking at the way that Paul has recorded and presented his ideas and thinking, what teaching could have helped him to communicate more effectively?
How could Paul have been encouraged to evaluate his project in relation to the original brief?

Assessment 3

Paul showed evidence of a range of decisions and a working knowledge of materials for producing his thermometer mounting. In his final evaluation insufficient emphasis was placed on how his solution meets his original needs. This may be because Paul's early work did not sufficiently identify real needs for him to see these as an essential element in achieving a successful outcome.
(Evidence of Tes 2.5d, 3.5a, 3.5b, 3.5d, 4.4a, 4.4b, 4.5b.)

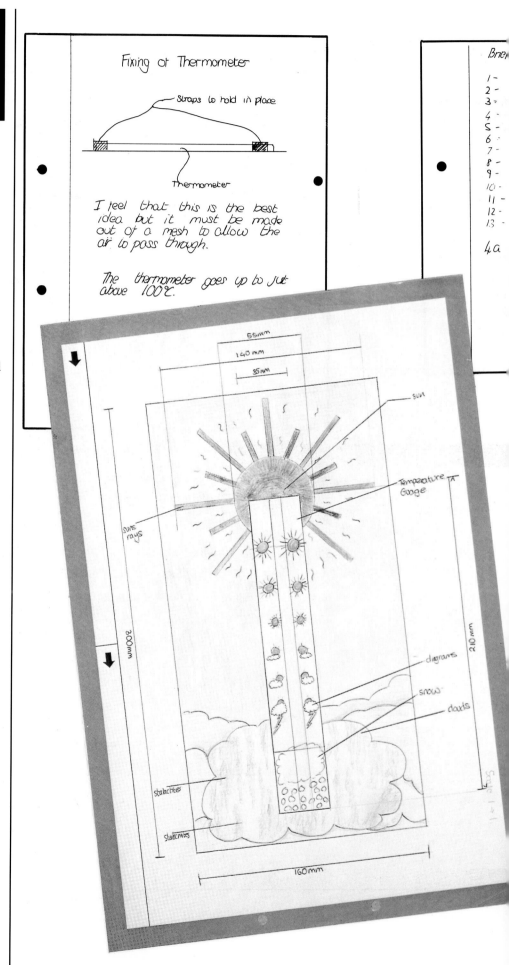

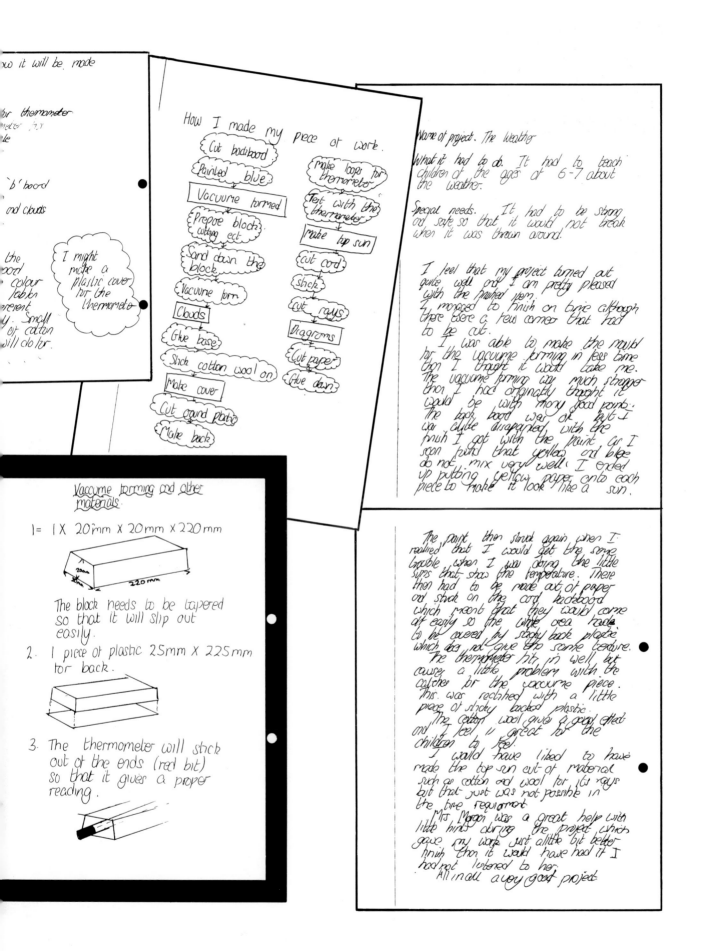

...ow it will be made

...or thermometer
...meter for
...le

..'b' board

...and clouds

...the
...ood
...colour
...table
...erent
...y. Small
...of cotton
...ill do for.

I might make a plastic cover for the thermometer

How I made my piece of work.

Cut backboard →
Painted blue →
Vacuume formed →
Prepare block, cutting ect →
Sand down the block →
Vacuume form →
Clouds →
Glue base →
Stick cotton wool on →
Make cover →
Cut round plate →
Make back

Make loops for thermometer →
Test with the thermometer →
make top sun →
Cut cord →
Stick →
Cut rays →
Diagrams →
Cut paper →
Glue down

Name of project. The Weather

What it had to do. It had to teach children of the ages of 6-7 about the weather.

Special needs. It had to be strong and safe so that it would not break when it was thrown around.

I feel that my project turned out quite well and I am pretty pleased with the finished item. I managed to finish on time although there were a few corners that had to be cut. I was able to make the mould for the vacuume forming in less time than I thought it would take me. The vacuume forming was much stronger than I had originally thought it would be with many good points. The back board was ok but I was alittle disapointed with the finish I got with the paint. As I soon found that yellow and blue do not mix very well. I ended up putting yellow paper onto each piece to make it look like a sun.

Vacuume forming and other materials.

1= 1 X 20mm X 20mm X 220mm

The block needs to be tapered so that it will slip out easily.

2. 1 piece of plastic 25mm X 225mm for back.

3. The thermometer will stick out of the ends (red bit) so that it gives a proper reading.

The paint then struck again when I realised that I could get the same trouble when I was doing the little slips that show the temperature. These then had to be made out of paper and stuck on the cord backboard which meant that they would come off easily so the white area had to be covered by sticky back plastic which did not give the same texture. The thermometer fits in well but causes a little problem with the catches for the vacuume piece. This was rectified with a little piece of sticky backed plastic. The cotton wool gives a good effect and I feel is great for the children to feel. I would have liked to have made the top sun out of material such as cotton and wool for its rays but that just was not possible in the time requirement. Mrs Morgan was a great help with little hints during the project which gave my work just alittle bit better finish than it would have had if I had not listened to her. All in all a very good project

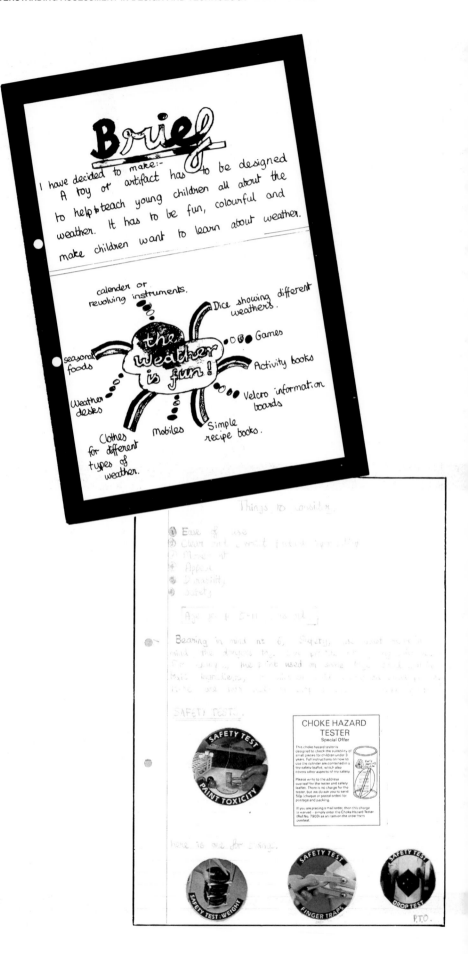

WORKING WITH RESISTANT MATERIALS

LEVEL 6
THEME: WEATHER
CONTEXT: SCHOOL
PROJECT: DRESSING TEDDY
PUPIL: JANE

Getting started

Aim

This group had previously worked on a project making moving toy vehicles, where the emphasis was in recording the process and the difficulties in planning and making. They had also worked on a food project where the main focus was the consumers' needs. The teacher planned these projects to develop pupils' strengths so they would be able to produce well-rounded and documented project work here. Equal emphasis was placed on the user's needs and the process of design and construction of pupil's design.

Assessment 1

Jane used systematic techniques to explore and research playing, toys and the child, teacher and retailer needs. She managed to reach conclusions about what toys should be like if they are to teach children about the weather successfully. *(Evidence of Tes 1.6a, 2.6c, 3.6e.)*

My questionaire

is a questionaire for teachers at the
school   who teach
geted age group, 5 year - olds.

u teach the children about the weather.
do.

o you do it - do you use any teaching

n them the basic water cycle I dont use
g aids
u think that children like colourful toys?
efinitely. They have to be attractive.
u think that children like to participate
lessons ?
definitely

it be better for the children to have
things of soft things to play with.
t matter really, as long as their colourful.

o children respond to different toys
enjoy toys that move or they can fiddle

do you think would attract children
rn about the weather?
e to learn about different clothes for different
, and it has to be fun.

Questionaire

1 I went to Brent Cross and asked an assistant
in the Early Learning Centre the following questions:
1, What age do you cater for?
from about two to ten years.
2, Do you have any toys in here which will
help children learn about the weather.
Yes

3, If you have, give a few examples.
We only have one activity book called "The weather"
4, Do these toys sell well?
About average
5, What tips can you give us if we were
designing something that would help children
learn about the weather ?
make it colourful.

6, What materials are best for making an object
for young children ?
soft materials. Something long-lasting I think.

7, What age do you personally think that children
should start learning about the weather ?
Erm, about 3, or later. First they could
learn basic things, then la...

Pupil Questionaire.

Have you ever learnt about the weather
at school ?
No
If so, what did you learn ?
_____

What is your favourite weather?
Sunny
Why?
Because at school we can go out to play And its
boring just staying inside.
Do you know what different clothes to wear
when it snows, when it rains and when
it is sunny ?
Yes
Do you like colourful toys ?
Yes
What are your favourite colours ?
black and white and red
In general, do you prefer hard or soft
toys ?
Soft toys.

CONCLUSION FOR INTERVIEWS.

From each interview, I found out something.
Some information was useful, but I already
knew most of it.

Here is why I chose to do the three
interviews:-

Teacher = Because she comes in close contact
with children all the time. She also
knows what they enjoy doing, and
what type of toys they prefer.

Child = Because the toy must appeal to
children, and talking to one would
give me ideas of what features it
should have.

Toyshop = I wanted to find out about products
teaching about the weather already on
the market, and if they sold well.

One thing I found from all three interviews, was
that children prefere soft and colourful toys.
This is good, because my idea includes both of
these. I think the best interview was the one
with the teacher, for I learnt the most. The least
best interview was with the Early Learning
centre, for the answers were predictable, and
I didnt learn anything.

WORKING WITH RESISTANT MATERIALS

LEVEL 6
THEME: WEATHER
CONTEXT: SCHOOL
PROJECT: DRESSING TEDDY
PUPIL: JANE

Developing ideas

Teacher's comments

Jane, a capable and resourceful pupil, managed to produce a project under adverse conditions. The problem was that the groups were timetabled in a resistant materials workshop, but Jane was convinced that her design must be produced mainly using felt. So she worked largely independently, with occasional reference to a textiles teacher. Jane has produced a well-documented account of her ideas, thoughts and working, using the fruits of her systematic research to inform the detail of her ideas. She also used her research to select and monitor her actions in achieving a successful outcome. The only thing the project lacks is a more complete report on consumer testing.

Assessment 2

Jane used her research to identify issues and to explore existing toys that could be modified and adapted to teach about the weather. She has briefly presented a number of ideas and supported these with explanations and criticisms of their suitability. Her reviewing skill enabled her to pick on a source idea 'fuzzy felt' to adapt as her teaching toy. *(Evidence of Tes 1.6a, 2.6a, 2.6b, 2.6c, 2.6d, 3.6e.)*

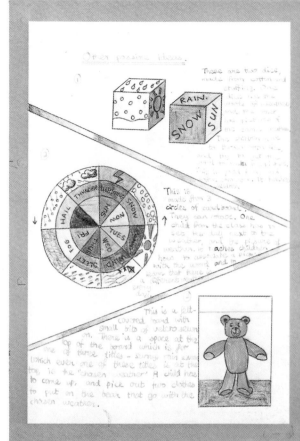

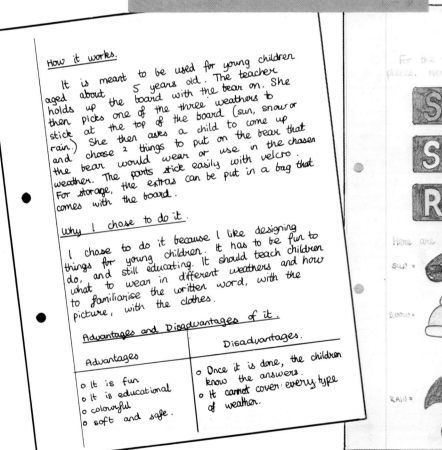

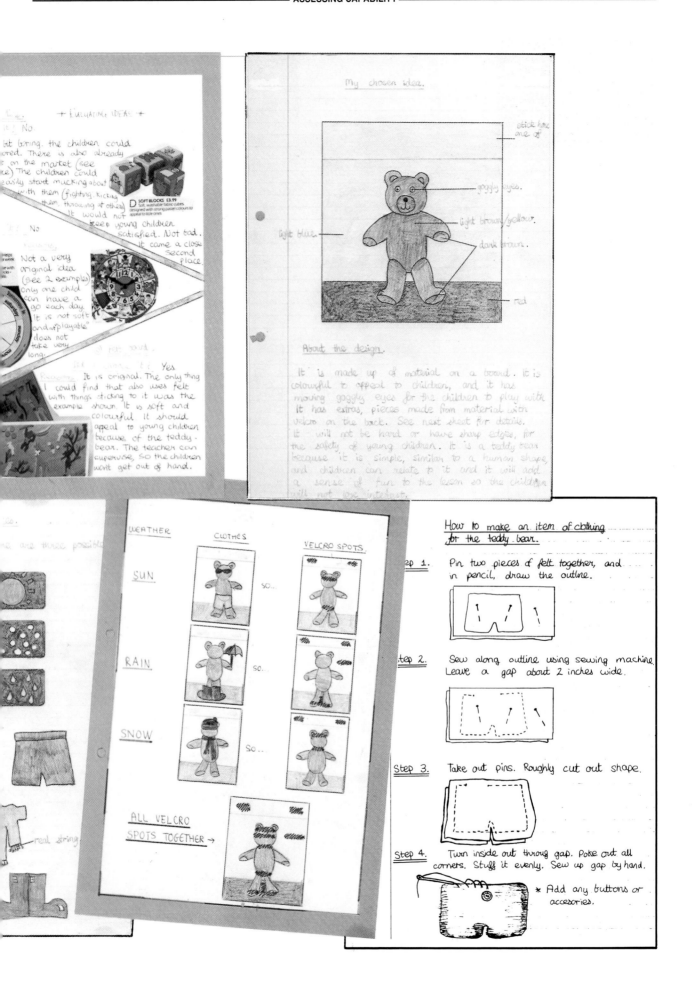

My chosen idea.

stick here one of

goggly eyes.

light brown/yellow.

dark brown.

light blue.

red

About the design.

It is made up of material on a board. It is colourful to appeal to children, and it has moving goggly eyes for the children to play with. It has extras, pieces made from material with velcro on the back. See next sheet for details. It will not be hard or have sharp edges, for the safety of young children. It is a teddy bear because it is simple, similar to a human shape, and children can relate to it and it will add a sense of fun to the lesson so the children will not lose interest.

EVALUATING IDEAS

No

... bit boring. the children could ...ored. There is also already ... on the market (see ...e) The children could ...easily start mucking about ... them (fighting, kicking ...them, throwing at others) ... It would not ...eep young children satisfied. Not bad. It came a close second place.

No

Not a very original idea (see 2 examples) Only one child can have a go each day. It is not soft and "playable" does not take very long.

Yes

Reasons: It is original. The only thing I could find that also uses felt with things sticking to it was the example shown. It is soft and colourful. It should appeal to young children because of the teddy bear. The teacher can supervise, so the children won't get out of hand.

WEATHER	CLOTHES	VELCRO SPOTS
SUN		so...
RAIN		so...
SNOW		so...

ALL VELCRO SPOTS TOGETHER →

real string

How to make an item of clothing for the teddy bear.

Step 1. Pin two pieces of felt together, and in pencil, draw the outline.

Step 2. Sew along outline using sewing machine. Leave a gap about 2 inches wide.

Step 3. Take out pins. Roughly cut out shape.

Step 4. Turn inside out through gap. Poke out all corners. Stuff it evenly. Sew up gap by hand.

* Add any buttons or accesories.

WORKING WITH RESISTANT MATERIALS

LEVEL 6
THEME: WEATHER
CONTEXT: SCHOOL
PROJECT: DRESSING TEDDY
PUPIL: JANE

Making things happen

Project review

How effectively did Jane use her research findings during her project?
How would you have intervened to help her make a more complete consumer test?
What aspects of prior knowledge and understanding (from the Programme of Study) has Jane demonstrated in her project?
Pupils at level 6 are expected to produce increasingly high-quality work and outcome. What evidence of this do you see in Jane's work?
What would you do to encourage pupils at this level to provide evidence of their concern for quality in their work?

Assessment 3

There is considerable evidence of what was to be done, what was done and Jane's problems and decisions in producing her toy. There is little evidence of how she tested her toy, the conclusions she reached and her improvements in the design (rather than the making).
(Evidence of Tes 3.6a, 3.6c, 3.6d, 3.6e, 4.6b, 4.6c, 4.6d.)

I have learnt how to organize myself more, including my time & my work. I have learnt practical skills, such as; using a machine accurately, making small cushions, sewing on buttons and how to stuff things equally.

I am good at doing + collecting research, choosing the colours and designing it.

To make it better, I should have made more patterns and done it better. I also should have done more sewing by machine, and used a pencil to mark the felt before sewing on it.

My research helped me think about the different possabilities of consider what types of weather to use, and what 5 year olds learnt about this by interviewing a 6-year old. By looking the toy must have some essentials. eg. colour, simplicity to

If I did the project again, I would make the whole thing from increasing in weight, I would not use chipboard for a lighter wood. If it was bigger, the children could easily gr be less fiddly. I had originally planned it to be much sm and made it bigger. I also changed the colour of the backg go, and there wasn't enough material

The project has turned out the same as I had planned. It h taken longer than planned. I think the results would have bee all bigger. b) If I had done more of the sewing by machine e no neater, and much quicker. Overall the results are good, as old children play with it.

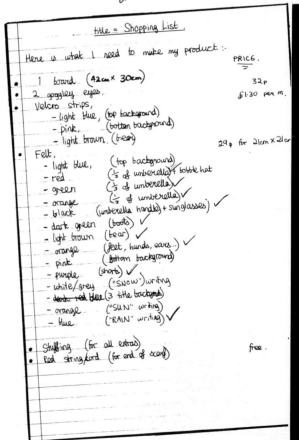

title = Shopping List.

Here is what I need to make my product :-

PRICE.

- 1 board (42cm × 30cm) — 32p
- 2 goggley eyes. — £1.30 per m.
- Velcro strips,
  - light blue, (top background)
  - pink, (bottom background)
  - light brown. (bear) — 29p for 21cm × 21cm
- Felt,
  - light blue, (top background)
  - red (⅓ of umberella + bobble hat) ✓
  - green (⅓ of umberella) ✓
  - orange (⅓ of umberella)
  - black (umberella handle) + sunglasses) ✓
  - dark green (boots)
  - light brown (bear) ✓
  - orange (feet, hands, ears...) ✓
  - pink (bottom background)
  - purple (shorts) ✓
  - white/grey ("SNOW") writing
  - ~~dark red~~ blue (3 title backgrnd)
  - orange ("SUN" writing)
  - blue ("RAIN" writing) ✓
- Stuffing (for all extras)
- Red string/cord (for end of scarf) — free.

Problem

Velcro is made up of

My original idea involved
sewn discreetly on to the
(eg boots, umberellas etc..)
the material - coated-board
words the felt would take

Unfortunately, there i
The loops must be stron
every time the two are
the hooks weaken the lo
creating a 'fluff' that doe

I thought about th
I should not try to fight
the substitute for the loops
the loops would lose their
aims of this toy is for it
long time without breaking.

... do. It made me
... e able to do. I
... alogues, I learnt that
... able etc...

... arger. To stop it
... rd, I would find
... ieces and it would
... I developed the idea
... ecause it ~~g~~ didn't

... e results, but has
... if a) I had made it
... it would have been
... ry letting some 5-year

... ooks.

... oops.

... ook parts'
... xtra pieces
... stick to
... elt) In other
... the loops.
... velcro, it is:
... hooks, or else
... m eachother,
... them, therefore

... decided that
... use felt as
... a few uses
... ll - one of the
... and last a

Now I have the problem that when I sew the loops onto the felt-covered-board, the bits of velcro would be very conspicuous, as velcro does not come in the colours I had originally planned. I had to choose the colours of the board to suit the colours of the velcro, and not choose the colours of the velcro to suit according to what colour the board would be. This meant a slight colour change, but no real problem.

SEWING

In my project, I used two types of sewing, machine sewing and Hand sewing. They both have advantages and disadvantages.

MACHINE SEWING
Ads = Very quick, neat, straight lines, easy.
Disads = Not much control on direction.

HAND SEWING
Ads = Accurate, good controll.
Disads = Not neat, can go wonky, slow, lot of concentration

I did some of my project in both.

MACHINE	HAND.
sewing on letters sewing clothes together sewing backgrounds large clothes eg. shorts, sewing on velcro. long, straight divider line.	small parts- eg. eyes any fiddly corners. most clothes sewing up all extras after they had been stuffed.

Flow Chart for next ten sessions

Session	Aims.
1	Finish three ideas sheet and collage of weather.
2	'Reasons why I didn't choose other 2' + velcro areas.
3	Problem with felt + velcro
4	Decide exactly what materials to use.
5	Start collecting materials (felt, velcro, board, eyes) Decide exactly what size everything will be.
6	Make board, and eyes on it. Decide stitches
7	Make board, and eyes on it.
8	Finish board, and start on clothing pieces.
9	Carry on with clothes and do top pieces (sun, rain)
10	Finish whole board + pieces. Test. Evaluate.

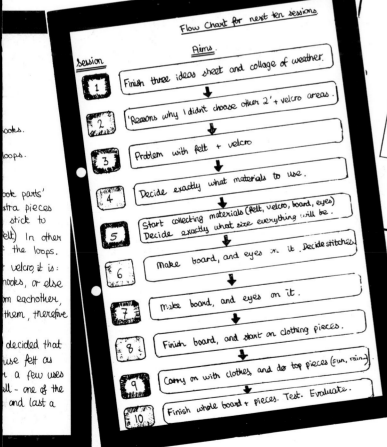

WORKING WITH RESISTANT MATERIALS

LEVEL 7
THEME: WEATHER
CONTEXT: SCHOOL
PROJECT: TEACHING AID
PUPIL: KAMAL

Getting started

Aim

This group had a considerable range of experience in using their technical understanding to develop ideas that work. They had less experience in designing for specified users. This project was set up to give pupils a real experience of a need (through visiting a local primary school). They were asked to regard the teacher and her pupils as their clients, whose needs had to be taken into account in their design work. Pupils would present their work to the school - so gaining a real insight into the success of their work.

Assessment 1

Kamal has explored the context and task - thinking about the teacher and the children's needs, the form and nature of weather information, symbols to represent the weather, display techniques - as well as coming up with several early ideas.
(Evidence of Tes 1.7a, 1.7b, 1.7c, 1.7d, 2.7a.)

THEME   THE WEATHER

A school wishes to establish a system for monitoring the weather. It is important that any display is relevant to the age range of pupils. What ideas could form part of their system?

'BRAIN STORMING'

rain gauge
LOR display
moisture sensor
light sensor
weather vein
big display for young children
(flashing) lights
sound?
cartoon character - like weather symbols.
symbols sticking out like a pop-up book
acid rain testing using a kit, litmus paper
a dial
big meshing gears
many gears to make the device look complicated and have
a window in the machine so the meshing gears show through
safety with the user
a help to the teacher which is a teaching aid
a device which uses little electricity - economical
age range - 4 to 7 year olds.
big handles - easy for youngsters to use

When watching television, I have noticed that there is usua... photograph. By introducing this s... to the children, I hope to mak... the things they see in the cla... things they experience in the re... this is very exciting for sm... children who cannot read o... are able to understand what ... gives the children great hapiness.

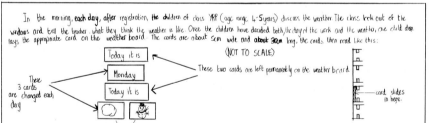

In the morning, each day, after registration, the children of class YRP (age range 4-5years) discuss the weather. The class look out of the windows and tell the teacher what they think the weather is like. Once the children have decided both, the day of the week and the weather, one child displays the appropriate card on the weather board. The cards are about 5cm wide and about 32cm long. the cards then read like this:

(NOT TO SCALE)

Today it is

Monday

Today it is

These 3 cards are changed each day

These two cards are left permanently on the weather board.

card slides in here.

These two cards together mean that it is cold and cloudy

One thing that I must remember is that the children can hardly read and that they are only used to very simply printed letters (see the photocopies of weatherboard cards following).

I used this particular idea because it would be practical and realistic to make in the time available. The ide... weather symbols appealed to me. I made a steering wheel to give the children enjoyment out of turning like things which are related to the the real world - so a steering wheel gives the idea of a car or some... irregularly shaped and is not flat - this helps the children develop their imagination. The children may also the steering wheel - which in turn turns the disc - rather than just turning the disc manually. The steering system which should not be too complicated to make. I have looked at scope for improvement in the m...

am making the dev...
things on it. If on...
good and it looked like...
work and -I rejecte...
have chosen seems reason...
first ideas - in rough...
It was a rack and pin...

Idea for BRIEF (A)

A device is needed for 5-7 year old children to display the weather. The device must be interesting, fun to use, and a safe teaching aid.

Idea for BRIEF (B)

A device is needed to display the weather. 5-7 year old children are using it. The device should be interesting. The device should not be unsafe for the children. The device should be a help to the teacher. The children should learn from it.

I think I will choose BRIEF(A) because it says everything that BRIEF(B) says but it is a lot more concise. Extra details, such as the environment where the device will be used and physical details of the children, eg. height etc. will be included in the research and specification.

RESEARCH POINT

I asked the teacher of the reception class I am studying (age range 4-5yrs) how much her school would be happy to spend on a weather display device which satisfies my chosen brief, she told me the school would not spend more than 20 pounds. This gives me another restriction for my brief:

NEW BRIEF

A device is needed for 5-7 year old children to display the weather. The device must be interesting, fun to use, a safe teaching aid and should cost no more than 20 pounds.

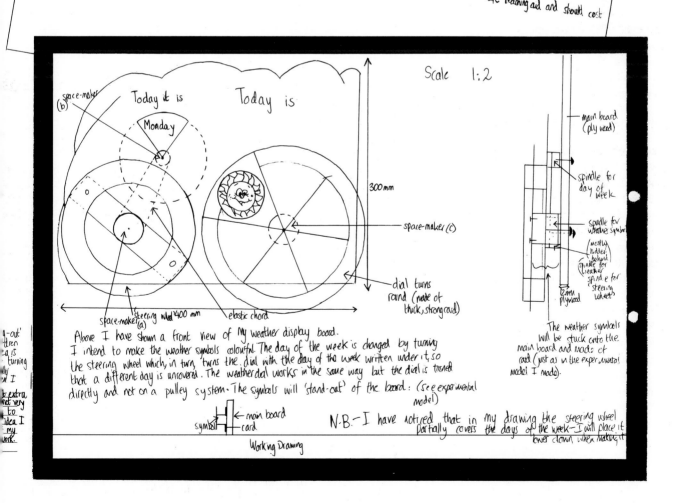

Above I have shown a front view of My weather display board. I intend to make the weather symbols colourful. The day of the week is changed by turning the steering wheel which, in turn, turns the dial with the day of the week written under it, so that a different day is uncovered. The weather dial works in the same way but the dial is turned directly and not on a pulley system. The symbols will 'stand-out' of the board: (see experimental model)

N.B.-I have noticed that in my drawing the steering wheel partially covers the days of the week-I will place it lower down when making it.

Working Drawing

WORKING WITH RESISTANT
MATERIALS

LEVEL 7
THEME: WEATHER
CONTEXT: SCHOOL
PROJECT: TEACHING AID
PUPIL: KAMAL

Developing ideas

Teacher's comments

Kamal is a thoughtful and thorough pupil. He approached his project in a thorough and systematic way that served him well in developing a range of creative and interesting potential solutions, and in detailing the decisions and concerns required to make one work. Given more time I would have liked to see him working with more resilient materials, rather than the card used for the dials, and for him to have time to work to a higher quality of finish on the product.

Assessment 2

These early ideas are explored and developed creatively through suggestions for interactive methods of displaying several types of matched information. Kamal drew on considerable mechanical understanding and proposed clear and workable possibilities. Each idea has some explanation of how it will be used and what it does, and there is a clear evaluation of the criteria for selecting and developing further the proposed idea.
(Evidence of Tes 1.7b, 2.7a, 2.7b 2.7c, 3.7c.)

In this idea I have tried to overcome the 'regularity' of a teaching aid. The layout is a lot more informal and colourful, make the device interesting. The day is adjusted by moving the long strip along and the weather symbols are on a visible one at a time.

ALTERNATIVE IDEA — 2

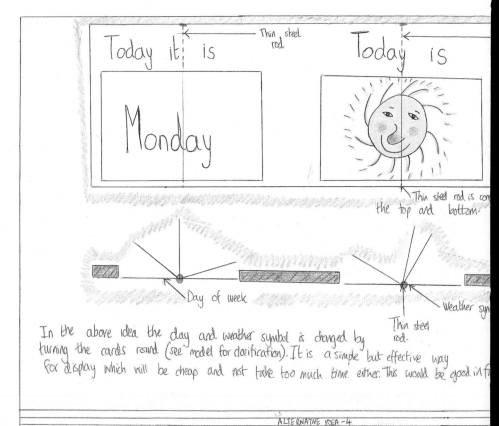

In the above idea the day and weather symbol is changed by turning the cards round (see model for clarification). It is a simple but effective way for display which will be cheap and not take too much time either. This would be good in f...

ALTERNATIVE IDEA — 4

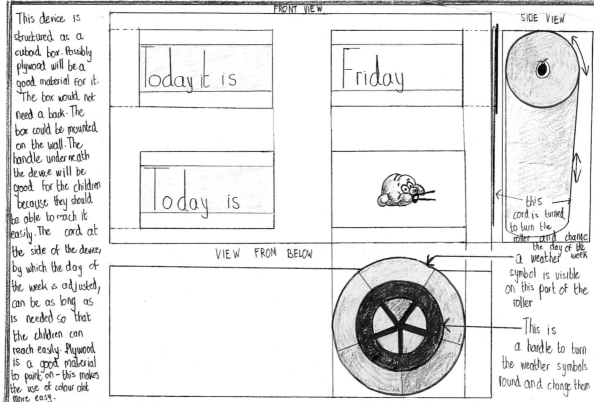

This device is structured as a cuboid box. Possibly plywood will be a good material for it. The box would not need a back. The box could be mounted on the wall. The handle underneath the device will be good for the children because they should be able to reach it easily. The cord at the side of the device, by which the day of the week is adjusted, can be as long as is needed so that the children can reach easily. Plywood is a good material to paint on - this makes the use of colour alot more easy.

FRONT VIEW

Today it is

Friday

Today is

SIDE VIEW

this cord is turned to turn the roller and change the day of the week

a weather symbol is visible on this part of the roller

VIEW FROM BELOW

This is a handle to turn the weather symbols round and change them

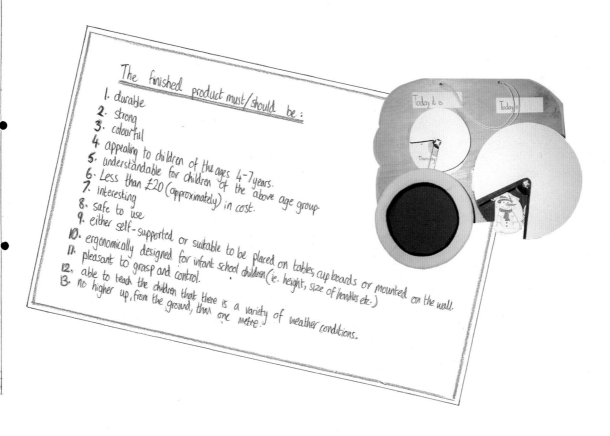

The finished product must/should be:

1. durable
2. strong
3. colourful
4. appealing to children of the ages 4-7 years.
5. understandable for children of the above age group.
6. Less than £20 (approximately) in cost.
7. interesting
8. safe to use
9. either self-supported or suitable to be placed on tables, cupboards or mounted on the wall.
10. ergonomically designed for infant school children (ie. height, size of handles etc.)
11. pleasant to grasp and control.
12. able to teach the children that there is a variety of weather conditions.
13. no higher up, from the ground, than one metre.

WORKING WITH RESISTANT MATERIALS

LEVEL 7
THEME: WEATHER
CONTEXT: SCHOOL
PROJECT: TEACHING AID
PUPIL: KAMAL

Making things happen

Project review

How effective was Kamal's research in clarifying needs and opportunities?
What are the main weaknesses in this project and how would you have intervened to enable Kamal to avoid them?
How can you help pupils at this level produce high quality finished products?
What evidence is there of technical understanding applied in this project?
How would you teach pupils at this level about using value judgements and objective evidence in evaluations?

Assessment 3

Kamal has evaluated his thinking and ideas continuously but did not produce a sufficiently detailed final evaluation for a secure level 7. He did test the outcome but then did not really draw on the users' reactions in his appraisal.
(Evidence of Tes 2.7c, 3.7a, 3.7b, 3.7c, 4.7a, 4.7b, 4.7d.)

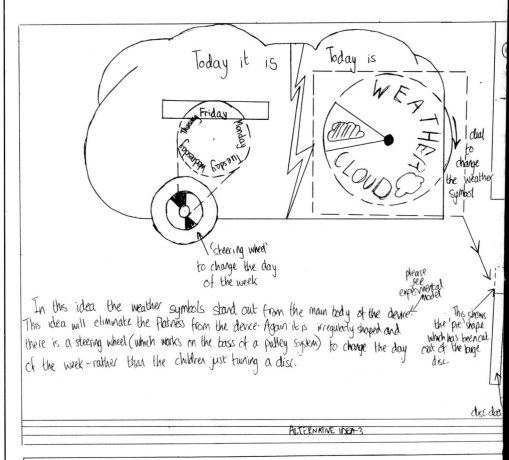

In this idea the weather symbols stand out from the main body of the device. This idea will eliminate the flatness from the device. Again it is irregularly shaped and there is a steering wheel (which works on the basis of a pulley system) to change the day of the week - rather than the children just turning a disc.

ALTERNATIVE IDEA-3

Parts List   Ø = diameter   All measurements are in MM

Part	Length	Width	Thickness	Material	Number	Cost (p)
Main board	400	300	12	Plywood	1	48
Wheel back	Ø = 180		3	Plywood	1	negligable
Steering wheel rim	Ø=180-Ø of 120 T=30			Plywood	1	210
Stopper on steering	Ø = 40		3	Plywood	1	negligable
Spacemaker (a)	20	Ø=40		Softwood	1	20
Spacemaker (c)	40	Ø=40		softwood		20
day-dial	Ø=120	X		Card	1	—
weather-dial	Ø=220	X		Card	1	—
weather symbols	Approx 40x40+40mm	X		Card	6	—
Spacemaker(b)	Ø20	20		Softwood	1	20

Total cost(p) £2.98
extras (nuts/bolts) negligable
Grand total £2.98

N.B- costing - a budget of ab that extras such a pens need not these are materials w

Order Of Manufacture

1. Cut out main board and mark out cloud shape- then cut it out
2. Draw a circle (diameter 120) and separate it into 5 equal segments (72° each segment) {See wor position
3. Write the day of the week the correct way up.
4. Cut out day-dial and space maker (b).
5. Cut one 72° segment out of the day dial.
6. Drill through the centre of the ?— spacemaker (b) and circle from number 2. Fix with nut and bo glue-on day dial onto space
7. Cut out wheel back and steering wheel rim. Fix them together
8. Attatch the complete steering wheel and spacemaker (a) to the weather board using a nut and bolt.
9. Cut out weather-dial & spacemaker (c). Glue together. Drill through centre
10. Drill through weather board (in the centre of a constructional 20cm diameter circle-see working drawing) and split into 6, 60°, segm
11. Make 6 weather symbols in same way as in experimental model, no bigger than the segments.
12. Attach weather-dial and spacemaker (c) to weather-board with nut and bolt.
13. Add words, colour and decoration where appropriate -using working drawing to help.

In my final design I needed to know how big the children's hands were. I found out that the children are only used to reading a particular style of reading. In my different ideas I tried to vary the ways of changing the display and I made models to test whether various methods of display would work. These experiments helped me to decide what sort of things would be realistic and practical under the circumstances. I saw that the current weather displaying system was not very absorbing - the children are likely to lose interest in it because it is regularly shaped and rather flat. This gave me ideas of using shapes related to the weather and used 'standing-out' weather symbols. I have realized that I need to find out the cost of the various materials and their durabilities so that when I work out the cost of my project I can evaluate whether the price is reasonable. For example, if my costing works out to less than £20 (my target) then it may still be expensive in the long run because the device may be very weak and need replacing very often.

I am doing the working drawing and I am thinking about all the dimensions and all the parts which move. I am going to use cork washers to keep the disc away from the actual device (see diagram) and I am making sure that the moving parts are strongly fixed. In all the handles steering wheel and the rotating dial I must always remember that the children are not used to fidgety little handles and are not very gentle with them. I am thinking about the properties of materials - for example I am going to use plywood for the main front because it needs to be strong. The front is going to be holding the whole device up and plywood is a material which is easy to work with as well. Plywood is a strong material. I will make the rotating discs out of thick card so that it is not floppy. Card is a good material to paint on or use other coloured materials on.

I still have to decide on how high up my weather display device should be display. I need to look at the heights and strengths of the children. I still need to decide how I will decorate the product and make it attractive to the children. I need to use techniques to catch the children's imagination. I have used techniques such as making the wind look like a person. I must look at the costs of various materials and so on because I have to work to a target of £20. This is why I have avoided using material such as acrylic. I also am constantly thinking about the long term cost - such as is it going to be replaced alot? If I have made an idea which will need to be replaced very often then it will work out to be too expensive in the long run.

---

symbols

surface is the weather symbol

surface s in the

other 3 dimensions (a)

positions may be stated

and disc parts

. This maintains required space the 2

TO WHAT EXTENT HAVE I FULFILLED MY BRIEF?

I have fulfilled every requirement in my brief. I have also, in view of the testing and teacher's comments, fulfilled all the aspects of my specification.

PROBLEMS IN MANUFACTURE

The steering wheel partially covered the days of the week, so I had to place it lower down on the device. I learnt the technique of using a lock-nut system, ie. using two nuts. This was because the dials got tighter every time they were turned clockwise and vice versa, so I put another nut on to keep the gap between the nut and device.

2nd nut which when tightened, stopped the nuts tightening, and untightening through use.

bolt

1st nut which kept moving

main device

The pulley-string on the day dial and steering kept slipping so I made grooves in the spacemakers to keep the string in the centre and the string had to be tightened. I also learned how to use a "jig" saw to cut out a circle in the steering wheel.

CHANGES MADE

I did not use a "cross-bar" on the steering wheel because I realized that it was not needed. Instead of writing words directly onto the wood I stuck card onto it - this was neater and it helped the writing stand-out more. I did not paint the main board because I saw that the natural wood was alot more suitable and the device had some character from it. I felt that if everything is painted the colours would 'clash', instead I picked out the "cloud-like edge" with yellow paint.

CHANGES I WOULD MAKE WHEN DOING THIS AGAIN

I would make the device at least twice as big in reality - because the writing, steering wheel and symbols would be much better if they were bigger. I would like to have more time so that I could tidy up things such as the inside rim of the steering - this is rather rough and uneven because there was not enough time to round it up nicely. I would make 2 sun symbols - one showing a cold scene, eg. a sun wearing a wooly hat. - and another with the sun sucking an ice cold drink. Also I would draw a clearer cloud on the rain picture because, when I was testing the device it often caused the children to ask questions. In my research, I found it very hard to find varying examples of weather display devices in schools. If there are already many existing devices, I would be pleased to see them because it would possibly inspire me to make something better than I have already made.

EVALUATION

WORKING WITH TEXTILES

LEVEL 3
THEME: ON THE MOVE
CONTEXT: COMMUNITY
PROJECT: RAINPROOF HAT
PUPIL: SIMON

Getting started

Aim

For pupils to achieve the learning aims described by the teacher:

Pupils may develop their skill in choosing appropriate materials through testing their properties (in particular, waterproofing and insulation).

The materials available were mainly unfamiliar and so I demonstrated working methods, which they would use in realizing their design.

Pupils have a chance to cut simple patterns for their designs, working from previous experience, or by modifying existing patterns and seeking help and advice. I felt it was important that pupils were guided, whilst they were developing their ideas, towards doing work that was within their capability, so that they were able to progress and achieve success.'

Assessment 1

Simon has recorded the task, and some brainstorming on types of weather and protective clothing, then jotted down early ideas for a porta welly and a hat with ear flaps and a neck guard.
(Evidence for Tes 1.3a, 1.3b, 2.3e.)

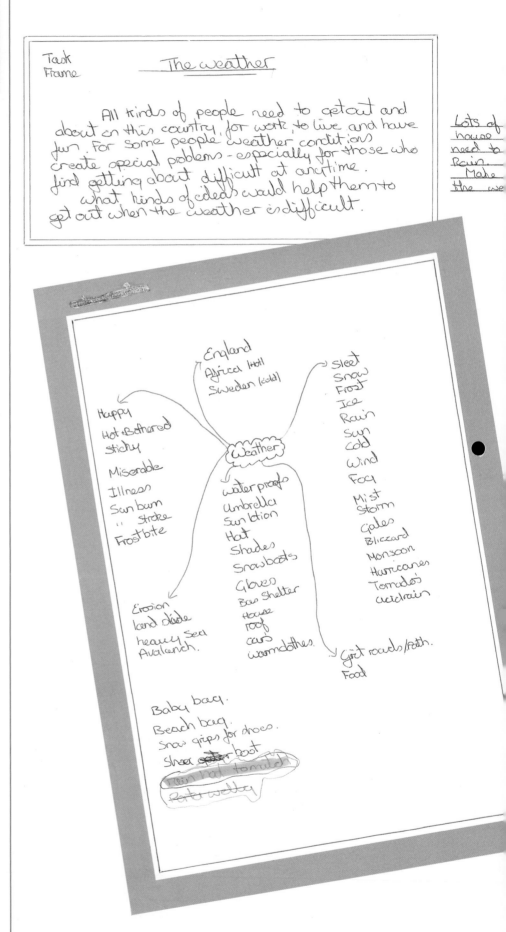

ed to get out of their
work purpose and fun. They
all kinds of weather fun—

to help the people when
ad (very sunny, raining) I will make
a rain hat.

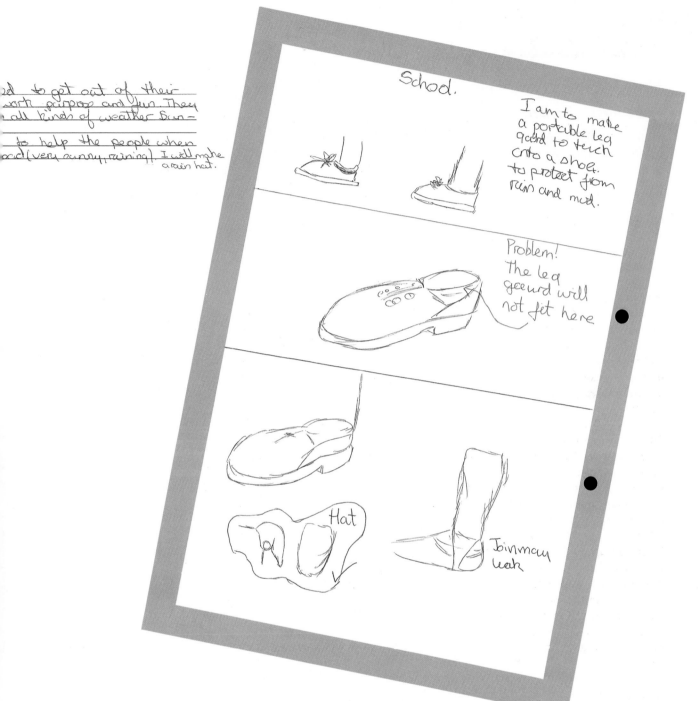

School.

I am to make
a portable leg
gard to tuch
onto a shoe.
to protect from
rain and mud.

Problem!
The leg
geeurd will
not fit here

Hat

Joinman
uah

I decided on my brief because lots of people (young-old) get wet when it
rains. My 'rain hat' is fold up and can be carried in your pocket. The hat will
protect your eyes from rain because of a peak, and it will stop rain going down
your neck.

Developing ideas

Teacher's comments

Simon used his own experience to come up with two early ideas, the 'porta welly' and a 'hat'. After talking over his ideas we agreed that he would develop the hat. Simon was very clear about what the hat would need to do and be like to be successful and he put his energy into making this happen. He looked at existing hats to get ideas for the pattern and I gave advice on how to take measurements. Despite having spent the majority of the time making his hat, Simon has not recorded much about the processes he used, nor how he chose the material. He was clear that colour was important and chose an olive green. He had some difficulty in machining the fabric, particularly the curves, and felt that he would not want to use such 'sticky' material again!

Assessment 2

Early in this phase Simon shows how he has used his experience to explain how his hat could meet people's protection needs from the rain, via a peak and flaps, as well as its benefit in being portable and fitting different head sizes. He has shown some simple sketches of how it can be worn and constructed. *(Evidence for Tes 1.3b, 2.3a, 2.3b, 2.3e, 3.3b.)*

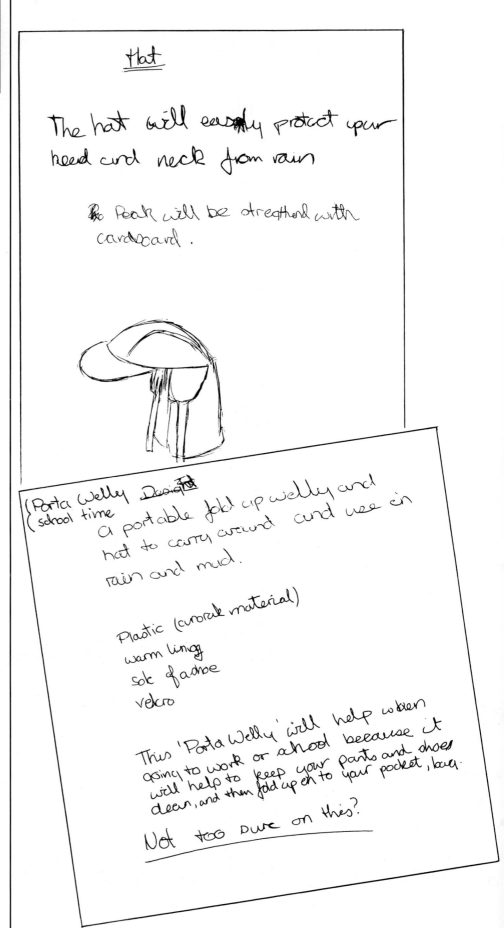

4 Stages of wear.

① ② ③ ④ ⑤

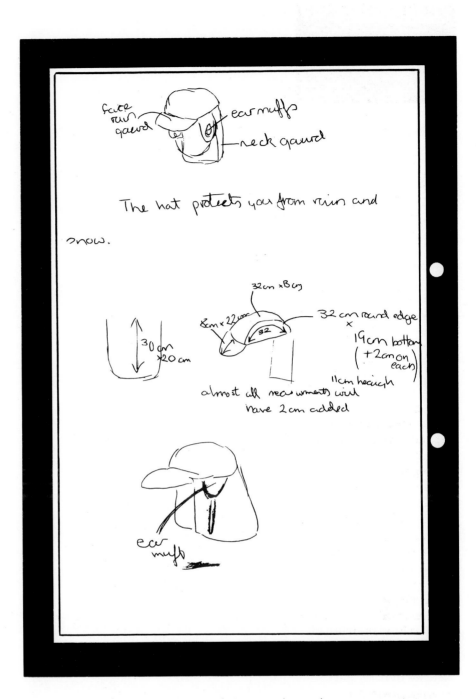

face rain gaurd — earmuffs — neck gaurd

The hat protects you from rain and snow.

32cm × 18cg
8cm × 22cm
32
30cm × 20 cm
32 cm round edge ×
19cm bottom (+2cm on each)
11cm heaich
almost all measurements will have 2cm added

ear muffs

I decided the Rain hat because lots of people catch head colds in rain, but the porta welley is good so you don't get your pants dirty (problem developed). So I chose the porta hat.

People's head are different sizes so the hat will have to be adjustable somehow by elastic or a fastener.
People will think it looks ridiculas so it well have to have variety on colours.
People will not be able to fasten it under their chun so I well have to think of a easy fastening system.

I will have to decide weather or not the hat will leak and that it won't shrink if I use some material. I will have to make it likeable.

WORKING WITH TEXTILES

LEVEL 3
THEME: ON THE MOVE
CONTEXT: COMMUNITY
PROJECT: RAINPROOF HAT
PUPIL: SIMON

Making things happen

Project review

How well do you think Simon managed to meet the teacher's aims?
What do you think Simon learned?
What previous experience do you think Simon would have needed to cope with this project?
How would you have intervened to ensure that Simon recorded more of what he was going to do, and had done?
Teaching for progression - how would you have structured the project or supported/guided Simon to make sure he achieved the next level?
What kinds of things would you plan into a future project to help a pupil at this level to progress?

Assessment 3

There is little evidence of how he made his idea happen, just rough sketches of parts and measurements. The finished hat shows some skill in machining and construction. His evaluation shows how pleased he is with his way of working, as he finished his hat within the time available. There is little consideration of how effective the hat was and how it could have been improved, except it would have been better if he had worked with wood!
(Evidence for Tes 3.3a, 3.3c, 3.3d, 4.3a, 4.3b.)

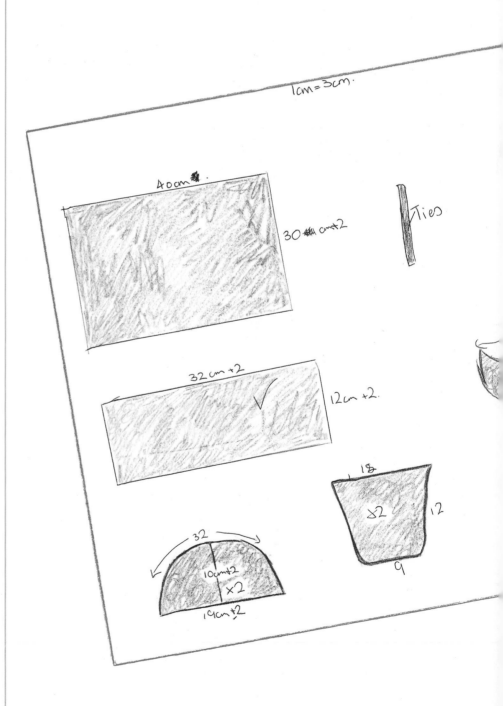

y research was enogh. It helped me decide on a handy thing
t will protect you from weather.

ped it as I did so my project would help people who need a hat to protect
om rain that can be pocket sized. If I did the project again I would try to
e materics like wood instead of material.

y planning was good because I fenished it in time and my making of
hat was easy and quick to do.
wouldn't plan it any different I planned it right.

My results are good and I had everything fenished so that was OK. I would
not change anything except the material I used, it tended to stick together
and not cut properly.

I have learnt to decide on a easy object
to make cheap and with no problems
I can do a few things well cooking, making
making objects Maths etc
I will make it easyer by using different materials.

WORKING WITH TEXTILES

LEVEL 4
THEME: KEEPING WARM
CONTEXT: HOME
PROJECT: DRAUGHT EXCLUDER
PUPIL: TINA

Getting started

Aim

Pupils worked within the theme of people's needs at home when the weather is bad. Early sessions were designed to help pupils (through discussion and stimulus material) to think about people's needs within a familiar context. They then would be able to identify a need or opportunity and an early idea for an artefact. Once pupils reached this point they were allocated to a room with suitable resources. The textiles teacher wanted to encourage pupils to use aesthetic values in developing and evaluating their ideas, as well as familiarizing them with the machinery available.

Assessment 1

Tina has a fairly clear idea of a number of things she could make, after an initial discussion. Her overview of making the draught excluder shows some knowledge of working with textiles. The problem of 'when is a context *familiar* or *unfamiliar*?' poses some questions for assessment. The teacher felt that her review of the context was mainly concerned with her own home, though her exploration covered the thinking and decisions to do with the unfamiliar problems of production. *(Evidence for Tes 1.3a, 1.4e, 2.4a.)*

DRAUGHT EXCLUDER

Reason: In the windy weather, our house get's dra[ught]
stop this problem.

Measurements: Length of door ____ M, ____ cm

Materials: cotton or felt, cardboard, felt, cotton woo[l]

Stages, how I am going to make it: Measure door —

→ stuff with cotton wool.

→ Piece of material (white) folded over and sown to the sausage shape to make the mouth:

white
mate[rial]
sown
sau[sage]

MILK BOTTLE HOLDER

Reason: In the windy weather the milk bottle
solve this problem.

Materials: Wood, nails, felt-tips.

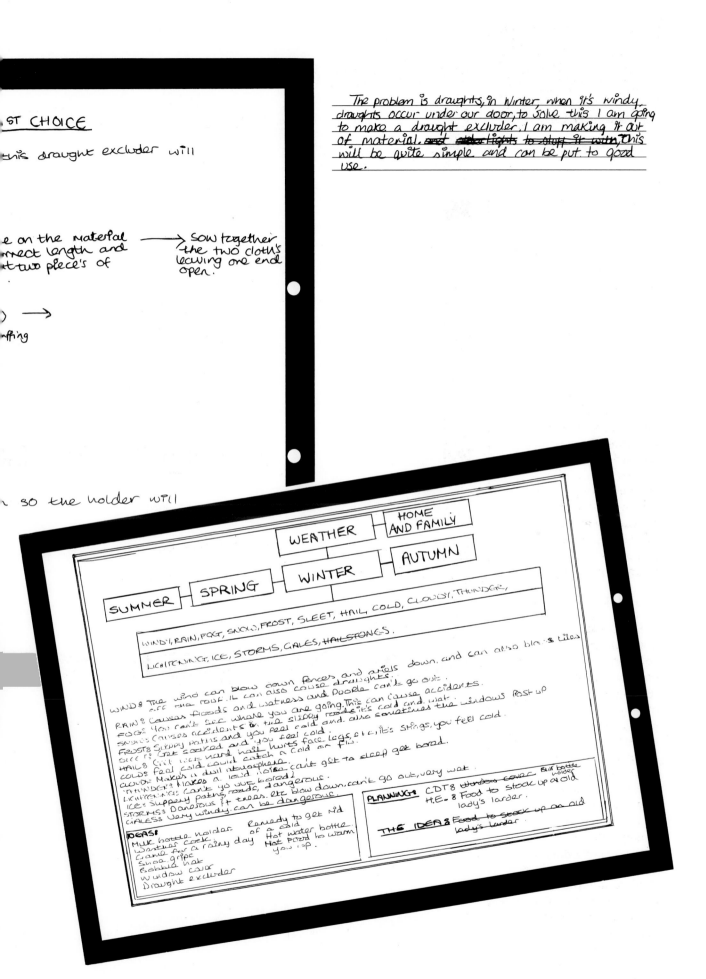

ST CHOICE

this draught excluder will

e on the material
rrect length and
t two piece's of

) ⟶

fing

⟶ sow together
the two cloth's
leaving one end
open.

n so the holder will

The problem is draughts, in Winter, when it's windy, draughts occur under our door, to solve this I am going to make a draught excluder, I am making it out of material. ~~and other lights to stop it with.~~ This will be quite simple and can be put to good use.

WEATHER
HOME AND FAMILY
AUTUMN
WINTER
SPRING
SUMMER

WINDY, RAIN, FOG, SNOW, FROST, SLEET, HAIL, COLD, CLOUDY, THUNDER,

LIGHTENING, ICE, STORMS, GALES, ~~HAILSTONES~~.

WIND8 The wind can blow down fences and ariels down, and can also blow tiles off the roof. It can also couse draughts.
RAIN8 Causses floods and wetness and Poorle can't go out. This can cause accidents.
FOG8 You can't see where you are going. This can cause accidents.
SNOW8 Causes acedents on the slippy roads its cold and wet.
FROST8 Slippy paths and you feel cold. also sometimes the windows Post up
SLEET8 Get soaked and you feel cold.
HAIL8 Get ice hard hail hurts face legs et cit's stings, you feel cold.
COLD8 Feel cold could catch a Cold or flu.
CLOUD8 Makes a dull atmosphere.
THUNDER8 Makes a loud noise, can't get to sleep get bored.
LIGHTENING8 can't go out bored.
ICE8 Slippery paths, roads, dangerous.
STORMS8 Dangerous if trees etc blow down, can't go out, very wet.
GALES8 Very windy, can be dangerous.

IDEAS8
Milk bottle holder   Remedy to get Rid
Weather Cock   of a cold
Game for a rainy day   Hot water bottle.
Shoe grips   Hot Pord to warm
Bobble hat   you up.
Window cover
Draught excluder

PLANNING8 CDT8 ~~Window cover~~ Buff bottle holder
H.E.8 Food to stock up old lady's larder.

THE IDEA8 Food to stock up on old lady's larder

Developing ideas

Teacher's comments

Tina worked very hard to achieve her finished draught excluder. She was able to continuously review her designing and making, taking into account her research on the appearance of crocodiles, and achieving an effective and appealing artefact. She is able to work consistently at level 4, but because her work was based around a familiar context 'the home' I felt uneasy about crediting Te1.4a, which requires an 'unfamiliar' context. Time also prevented Tina from testing her draught excluder and including this aspect in her evaluation.

Assessment 2

Tina's reports on her progress show that she was struggling with some unfamiliar processes in attempting to make her idea real. She communicates the progress of her ideas and in particular, an exploration into the appearance of crocodiles. My impression is of a pupil with a clear view of what her idea should be like to be successful and her struggle to make it happen. There is little detailed evidence of knowledge and understanding of the textiles' working, though this may be inferred from the quality of the product. *(Evidence for Tes 1.4b, 2.4a, 2.4b, 2.4c, 3.4d.)*

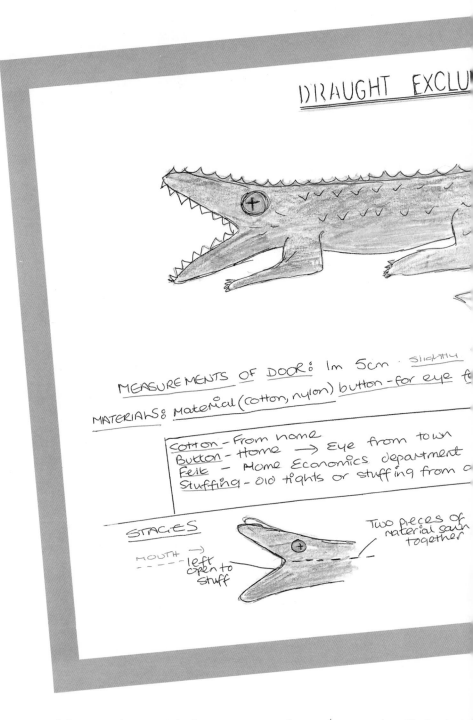

DRAUGHT EXCLU

MEASUREMENTS OF DOOR: 1m 5cm. slightly

MATERIALS: Material (cotton, nylon) button - for eye f

Cotton - from home → Eye from town
Button - Home Economics department
Felt - Home Economics department
Stuffing - old tights or stuffing from o

STAGES

MOUTH → left open to stuff

Two pieces of material sewn together

I chose the draught excluder because my other choices weren't very good. eg - The milk bott holder, I'm not very good with hammers and wood. Cooking - I wouldn't really know what to m weather cock - I wouldn't get it done in time. Game (board) - Many people were doing this. So, my idea of a draught excluder was the most sensable to make. I chose the crocodile a was more original than other peoples. peoples.

I will also have to learn rather quickly how to use the sewing mac as I have only used one once bef that was 3 years ago, I will need to learn again as I have forgotten.

I chose a crocodile because it is quite original as every one was either doing a snake or catupiller. I was looking through a book when I found the crocodile, I then had to look up so more information to see what they looked like, I knew more or less but there were so details that I wouldn't have put on my crocodile if I hadn't of looked at the book. eg the

I am making the draught excluder because it can be put to very good use and it will be quite simple to make. The materials will be easy to ~~find~~ provide, I have most of them at home, so I, or the school won't need to buy anything new, it will stop us getting draughts in winter.

These are all the idea's that I have had: A milk bottle holder, window cover, remedy to get rid of a cold, shoe grips, hot nurishing meal, gloves, ~~scarfs~~ scarves, some kind of soup and a game for a rainy day. I found it quite difficult to decide out of making a draught excluder or a milk bottle holder, in the end, I decided a draught excluder as it can be put to more use as our milk bottles are placed in a cubby hole ~~thing~~ so the wind doesn't blow them over that much, but we always get draughts under our door.

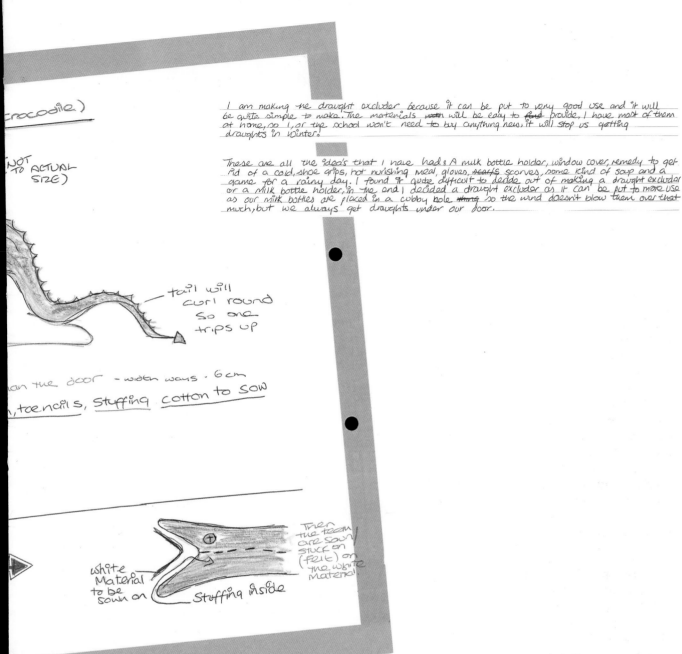

crocodile)

(NOT TO ACTUAL SIZE)

tail will curl round so one trips up

an the door - width ways. 6cm
, toenails, stuffing cotton to sow

white Material to be sown on   Stuffing inside

Then the ~~team~~ are sown stuck on (felt) on the white Material

After I have measured the door and measured the material, I then have the problem of sowing together the material, sowing by hand will take quite a while as it is a metre long, so I will probably use the sowing machine, so I will have to talk to the ~~the~~ teacher about ~~this~~. I then have the problem of stuffing down the stuffing down, right to the bottom, I will have left the top open so I will have to shove ~~the~~ stuffing down with a wooden pole, ~~of~~ or a ruler (metre), I will get ~~these~~ this from the C.D.T. department.

For a start my draught excluder would have to be sown good, to stay together, so it will work. It will also have to be the right size, I will measure my door to make sure. As if it is to small it ~~will~~ will not ~~work~~ work? Also, what about ~~the~~ other three sides? That is an important ~~descison~~ decision as I will have to work out which side it is for, I will make it for the side that has the biggest gap.

WORKING WITH TEXTILES

LEVEL 4
THEME: KEEPING WARM
CONTEXT: HOME
PROJECT: DRAUGHT EXCLUDER
PUPIL: TINA

Making things happen

Project review

Was this project a success in enabling pupils to identify needs and opportunities?
How else could pupils have been encouraged to research into people's needs at home in bad weather?
What else do you think Tina could have been taught?
Can you think of a way to rephrase the starting point to encourage pupils to look into unfamiliar contexts?
Teaching for progression - how would you have structured the project or guided Tina to make sure she achieved the next level?

Assessment 3

Tina was preoccupied with the way her crocodile would look and be made, rather than how effectively it keeps out draughts. At level 4 the evaluation needs to include more appraisal of her working process and more consideration of factors such as efficient use of resources, testing, or reference to other people's views.
(Evidence for Tes 2.4b, 3.4a, 3.4c, 3.4d, 4.4a, 4.3b.)

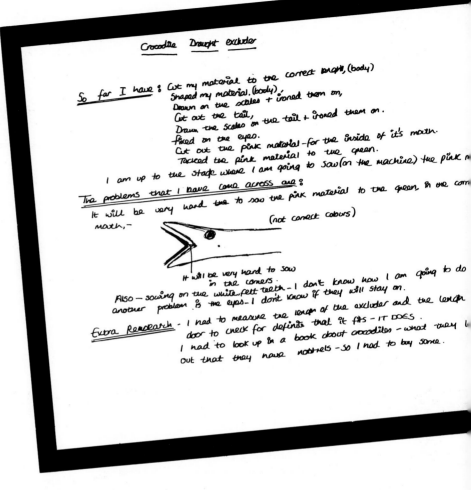

So far my crocodile is working – it's the right size and the eyes have stayed on. So far I have cut my material to the correct length, shaped the body, drawn + ironed on the scales (body) cut the tail, drawn and ironed on the scales on the tail, fixed on the eyes, measured and cut out pink material for it's mouth (inside), tacked the pink material to the body. I am now up to the stage of sowing (on the sowing machine) the pink material on to the green material (body). I also did some extra research when I looked up crocodiles in a book – I found out they had nostrils.

My crocodile is progressing fairly well, although we have only got 3 more lessons to go. I think I will get it finished, all I have to do is stuff the body + tail, sow up the tail and sow the in mouth (pink) to the outer mouth (green).
An important decision that I have to make is now I am going to sow on the tooth. big fierce, white, felt teeth and they will look good if I put them on properly, only I don't know how yet. It is important that I get them right, so they look good, it is one of the most important parts.

I have learnt that attaching the tail to my crocodile was alot harder than I to do the scales well on my crocodile.
I think, on my next project, I will work alot faster so my sewing isn't all rushed.
I have also learnt that I should have sown in the teeth with the mou as it took me alot long to make than it should have.

My draught excluder, I think, should keep out any draughts at all, as it is a large excluder, alot larger than I intended. When I think about it though, it has turned out better, because the length I intended ~~was too small~~ would be a bit small and thin.

I developed the idea to put scales on my crocodile, as I thought it made it look alot more ~~than~~ like a crocodile ~~than it did without scales~~.
If I did the project again I would sew the teeth in with the mouth, as I wasted alot of time sewing the teeth on seperately. I would also sew on the tail differently as my sewing was rather rushed at ~~the~~ end, I think I would be more careful. Also I think I would be more careful when stuffing my crocodile →

as in some places small lumps appeared, especially in the mouth.

My planning, I think, I couldn't do without, as I planned all the coloured materials I needed and also the features. If I hadn't planned, I would have forgotten all the things I needed. I think, I would plan the measurements a bit more carefully as my croc ended up rather on the large side, also my tail was a touch to small for my body, obviously my measurements were wrong, but in the end my tail looked alright as I tucked it inside my body.

I think my results were quite good. The body had scales, teeth, eyes and a tail which a crocodile has. I think if the sewing on the tail ~~were~~ wasn't as rushed the product maybe better and also if the teeth didn't stick out as much.
My crocodile maybe better if I'd have put a tounge on it, but unfortunatly I didn't have any time left.
Overall, I am pleased with my product and it will be put to good use.

CROCODILE

My main problem was how to put on the tail. My idea was to stuff the ends of the body into the tail, and sew, but this was not possible. In the end I decided to attach the tail onto the end of the body, making the edges neat.

sewing.

Just to finish it off, I decided to put on darker green scales which made it look more like a crocodile, as it was rather bare.

I really enjoyed making it, and the materials were not that expensive:

White felt for teeth : 18p.
Two eyes : 12p
Body + tail : Already had it
Inner mouth : Already had it,

I think my crocodile was fairly good, but there are some things that I should have done:
1. Sewn the teeth in with the material,
2. Worked a bit faster!

WORKING WITH TEXTILES

LEVEL 5
THEME: KEEPING WARM
CONTEXT: COMMUNITY
PROJECT: DRAUGHT EXCLUDER
PUPIL: GEOFF

Getting started

Aims

To promote an investigative design process taking account of the needs and opinions of elderly people in the community. Programme of Study focus:
- the diverse and changing preferences of consumers
and
- the impact of d&t activity on the environment.
Some understanding of techniques for saving and retaining energy was involved in the project as well as the development of an understanding of the relative insulating properties of materials.

Assessment 1

Geoff had some difficulty in deciding what to do, partly because of his lack of knowledge of working with textiles. He does 'invent', after much thinking and some consultation with the elderly people he meets on his paper round, an idea for a draught excluder. It is made out of blocks so that it will fit any door size. He does not work out what makes an effective draught excluder or consider whether elderly people would want a novelty-shaped one.
(Evidence for Tes 1.5a, 1.5b, 2.5b.)

Planning My Project

The important things in this project will be:
1) Deciding what to make, and whether or not it will fulfill its purpose.
2) Finding which materials are available to me, and adapting my to this if necessary.
3) Getting other peoples opinions on what I plan to make, and possibly using these views to alter my plans.
4) Making the object(s).
5) Evaluating what I have done, and seeing if any alterations c be made to improve the product.

Brief

Winter / summer can create difficulties for elderly people, so whom live alone, manage on a tight budget and have few of the k things that make life easy. What kind of ideas would help them l after their basic needs?

It seems to me that the basic problems which elderly people fa those of pure heat and / or cold, and the illnesses and allergi which are caused as a direct result of these conditions. The wir reports of older people dying of hypothermia in their own front appear to back this up. According to one of my teachers, a big is that these elderly folk find it almost impossible to differe between warm and cold weather, and in any case, their bodies react very fast to any changes in temperature. This would sugge that either the people themselves, or else their houses, need insulated in some way to keep what heat is already in the house and the cold out.

Of the vague ideas which I have considered, I think warm, outfits can be ruled out, since not very many elderly people very happy to wear that sort of thing. Wool is fairly warm, b the air trapped in it (see diagram below), so it may be that learn to knit...

Air is trapped in these wholes. It acts as a vacuum b body heat and outside air.

It seems that to solve the problem, either partially or completely, I have to go to the source of the problem — i.e. the old person. They would probably for more comfortable in warmer clothing, which would prevent heat from leaving their body, and also keep the cold out. Once the person was warm, then problem of keeping their dwelling warm could be addressed. After all, the warmth of their wallpaper doesn't really matter if the person is warm, because the p is the only thing needing protection.

The first thought that fingers and toes needed to be kept warm, but then realised that the big problem areas are the body and the head. Perhaps a all-over garment might work here — but I don't think too many old folk would be very keen on that. It seems to come down to normal garments being made from some sort of insulating material which will not be too hot, and will allow sweat to escape easily.

I am not very good at sewing or machine sewing, and so making clothes is going to be something of a tall order. It will mean that I will have to p and get a lot better at those skills. I will need to visit the library, the post office (to find out how much an average pension is; I don't want to c something costing ten pounds and find the old person only has 25p to spend on it.)

Cost the right amount for an old person. Be made of realistic things (i.e. it's no good if it's brilliant but made out of the wool of Lesser Spotted Arabian Be warm, and meet all briefs.

1) Old peoples extremities get cold. 2) They often don't realise the temperature of the room 3) They don't, on average, have much money. The ones I spoke to all preferred not to wear certain clothing, and all liked the idea of an adjustable draught excluder. One gentleman said he would love it if that kind of thing was in the shops. From the seven people I spoke to, five preferred the blocks, one the biscuits, and one the gold bar, although I think he was joking. Anyway, the outstanding vote was for the blocks.

I thought that, because extremities of an old person get cold quickly, I could make gloves or socks of some kind, but it didn't seem like old folk would want to wear a particular pair of gloves/socks all the time, as they might not be able to afford a second pair. The same (more or less) went for other items of clothing, which of course would have to vary in size for each person. Therefore it seemed that insulating the house would be better, and also letting the person see the temperature of their home. I invented a draught excluder which comes in velcro-edged segments, which would fit accross many widths of doors. One of the blocks would have a built in display thermometer.

I am now ready to begin manufacturing the draught excluder(s). The only problem I see at the moment is in-building the thermometer, and building it in safely so that when somebody treads on it (as they inevitably will) it will not leak mercury all over the floor. I have still to decide which material would be the best for excluding draughts. I will test this with a sample of the material and a hairdryer.

Decisions: 1) What material will I use (regarding availability, fire risks, weight, price, colour etc.) 2) Will the thermometer be safe in the blocks, or should it be wall-mounted? 3) What will I fit the blocks with? 4) The actual project can be a chronicle of these decisions and their results (or not.)

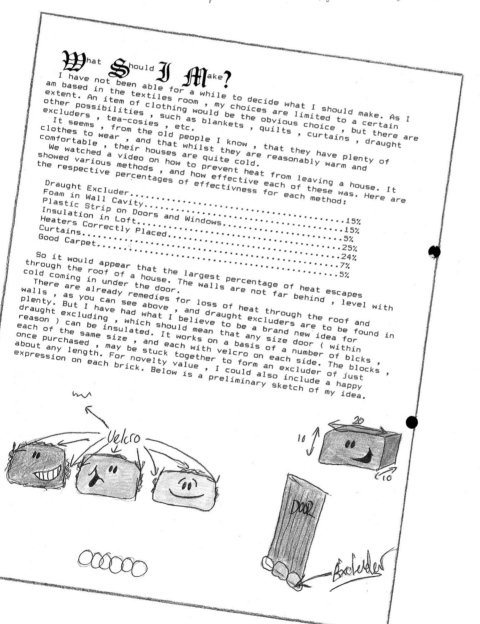

What Should I Make?

I have not been able for a while to decide what I should make. As I am based in the textiles room , my choices are limited to a certain extent. An item of clothing would be the obvious choice , but there are other possibilities , such as blankets , quilts , curtains , draught excluders , tea-cosies , etc.
It seems , from the old people I know , that they have plenty of clothes to wear , and that whilst they are reasonably warm and comfortable , their houses are quite cold.
We watched a video on how to prevent heat from leaving a house. It showed various methods , and how effective each of these was. Here are the respective percentages of effectivness for each method:

Draught Excluder...15%
Foam in Wall Cavity..15%
Plastic Strip on Doors and Windows...................5%
Insulation in Loft..25%
Heaters Correctly Placed.....................................24%
Curtains...7%
Good Carpet..5%

So it would appear that the largest percentage of heat escapes through the roof of a house. The walls are not far behind , level with cold coming in under the door.
There are already remedies for loss of heat through the roof and walls , as you can see above , and draught excluders are to be found in plenty. But I have had what I believe to be a brand new idea for draught excluding , which should mean that any size door (within reason) can be insulated. It works on a basis of a number of blcks , each of the same size , and each with velcro on each side. The blocks , once purchased , may be stuck together to form an excluder of just about any length. For novelty value , I could also include a happy expression on each brick. Below is a preliminary sketch of my idea.

velcro

DOOR

Excluder

WORKING WITH TEXTILES

LEVEL 5
THEME: KEEPING WARM
CONTEXT: COMMUNITY
PROJECT: DRAUGHT EXCLUDER
PUPIL: GEOFF

Developing ideas

Teacher's comments

Geoff is an able pupil with good communication skills which he used to advantage in gathering data on people's opinions and presenting his ideas and decision making. He was hindered by his lack of knowledge and experience of working with textiles. He managed his time well and achieved what he set out to do, but perhaps should have spent more time considering the concept of a number of blocks which join to form a draught excluder of a suitable length.

Assessment 2

Having finally decided to make a draught excluder he gives plenty of evidence for the ways he gathered users' opinions and preferences to enable him to make choices about his designs. This level of targeted research informing design work is typical of pupils working at level 5 and above. Some simple sketches are included recording the development of ideas, but the overall graphic skill level is not great.
(Evidence for Tes 2.5a, 2.5b, 2.5c, 2.5e, 3.5d, 4.5b.)

Size

Now I have decided what I am going to make , I must work out the dynamics of each of the blocks.
The width of a doorway may be anything between 50cm and 1 metre , but for the blocks to look any good , there must be at least three of them. Usually , house-doors average around 85-87cm. So if the bricks measured 18cm long each , five of them would insulate an average-sized door. So it is quite important to look like blocks , and not long flat slabs.
The blocks ought to make sure that they are high and deep as well as long. I think that 10cm each way would be quite good.

The Insulator

Although I have worked out which materials I am going to use , I have not yet thought of what stuffing I should use. This is possibly the single most important factor in the project.
I am unable to repeat the previous test for the stuffings; some are too expesive to buy a whole sheet , and some don't come in sheet form anyway. Below is a list of possible insulating materials.

Foam rubber — — — — — — — — — — probably not that good
Water — — — — — — — — — — — — — good but difficult to contain
Old stocking type stuff — — — — — best so far
Feathers— — — — — — — — — — — — probably very good
Compressed foam rubber — — — — — used in industry , very heavy
Sand— — — — — — — — — — — — — excellent but heavy

This is the result of pooling a classroom-full of knowledge. Things which strike me about this list straight awaay are as follows:
1) I believe feathers to be somewhat expensive.
2) Whatever is containing the water needs only to be damaged in some way , and you have no draught excluder , just a soaked carpet.
3) Foam rubber is not very good , since I can breath perfectly easily through it. Therefore draughts could do the same thing.
4) If there was such occurence as a fire , a very frail person could quite possibly not manage to lift a draught excluder which was filled with sand. The same might also go for the compressed foam rubber.

The only substance which would be left , was I to eliminate those materials in the problems section above , would be the 'scraps of almost any material' mixture (old stockings included). Whether this would be heavy enough to remain in place , I am not sure. Although as the bricks are to have flat sides on them , the likelihood is that they would remain where placed.
As a result of all the above information , I feel that I need only investigte the price of feathers , and see if my Mum is about to throw out any stockings.

Mat...
Althogh still ver these mat
As the the exclu allows le experimen

Exp...
Apparatus
Electri
Sheet o
Hand-he
Two Peo

Method:
One per
whilst t
of materi
large s
also hold
is of t
the fairg
mouth.
be start
material
thing di
See diag

Results:
The tw
these ,
brushed
the blue

Conclusi
The bl
choices

Colours

Now that I have picked the basic design , I must details , one of which is colour . Would a uniform block be best? Or maybe a different colour for eac two basic colours? Or three?
I have made a miniature sample booklet to show as the colour schemes available to me.

TOP
SIDE 1
SIDE 2
BASE
BACK

In most colours, the procedures may be reversed.

Of these colour sets , those made of randomly co material look rather tatty , at least on paper. In the sets which are made up intirely of one colour boring. To put it in short , my favourites are tho complimentry colours....

Blue..............strong , vibrant
White.............easily soiled
Red...............strong , bold
Yellow............gentle , possibly contrastin
Green.............soothing , considered unluck
Purple............warm , inviting
Brown.............warm , comfortable
Patterned.........adds interest , provides co

Continued on

amount of materials at my disposal , it is
pick the right stuff for the job. Most of
if that should be necessary.
rcise is to stop draughts from permeating
st of all test to see which of the materials
. For this , I have devised the following

ested

hairdryer ,
he sheet
reasonably
sed.   He
ng (which
u get   at
 in his
r   should
d at the
the whirly
ther side.

were brushed cotton and poly-cotton. One of
comes in a dark shade of blue , whilst the
green or white. Green looked terrible with
which was very clean , looked pretty good .

the white brushed cotton would be the best
available to me.

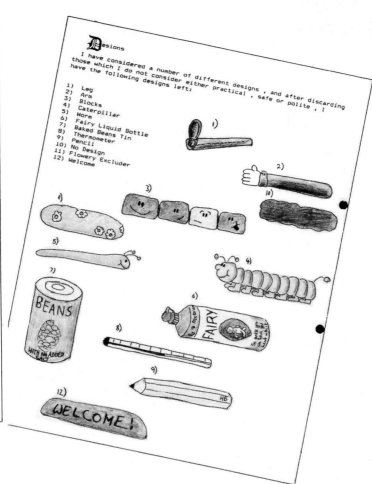

Designs

I have considered a number of different designs , and after discarding
those which I do not consider either practical , safe or polite , I
have the following designs left:

1) Leg
2) Arm
3) Blocks
4) Caterpillar
5) Worm
6) Fairy Liquid Bottle
7) Baked Beans Tin
8) Thermometer
9) Pencil
10) No Design
11) Flowery Excluder
12) Welcome

Opinions

1y paper-round is in streets inhabited almost entirely by older and
etired people. I took my sheet of designs to ten of these folk ,
including two married couples , and asked each person to firstly choose
the excluder which , in their opinion , looked the best as regarded
colour , style , etc , and secondly to choose the excluder which they
thought would do its job best and be practical to live with.
Here are the statistical results of this survey.

Design	Looks	Practical
Leg	0	0
Arm	0	0
Blocks	7	9
Caterpillar	0	0
Worm	0	0
Fairy Liquid Bottle	1	0
Baked Beans Tin	0	0
Thermometer	0	0
Pencil	1	1
No Design	0	0
Flowery Excluder	0	0
Welcome	1	0

Clearly my samplers considered the blocks to be good to look at , but
more importantly , practical to use.
Of the others which were voted for , the pencil was chosen because of
its shape , which was just right for the space to be filled. The Fairy
Liquid bottle was chosen for its looks , as was the 'Welcome' sign ,
although as the man who chose it pointed out , the 'Welcome' would be
on the wrong side of the door.
Regardless of that , the bricks certainly seem to be doing well on
the publicity side of things.

gn
to
of

WORKING WITH TEXTILES

LEVEL 5
THEME: KEEPING WARM
CONTEXT: COMMUNITY
PROJECT: DRAUGHT EXCLUDER
PUPIL: GEOFF

Making things happen

Project review

How could Geoff have been encouraged to build on his knowledge and understanding of textiles? An important aspect of Geoff's idea is that it is made of blocks or units, which can be joined to draught proof any size of door. He does not make more than one. How does this affect the success of his project?
Which aspects of the project are the weakest? Which are the strongest? How could his teacher have intervened to help him improve on his work? What aspects of the Programme of Study are shown in this project?

Assessment 3

Geoff made only one block, so was unable to test his system, which is a pity. Throughout the project Geoff evaluates his work in order to take decisions and plan. His final evaluation is mainly focused on the production of his design, though he does refer to the ways in which other people's opinions informed his idea. There is only just sufficient recorded evidence to achieve level 5. *(Evidence for Tes 2.5e, 3.5a, 3.5d, 4.5a, 4.5b.)*

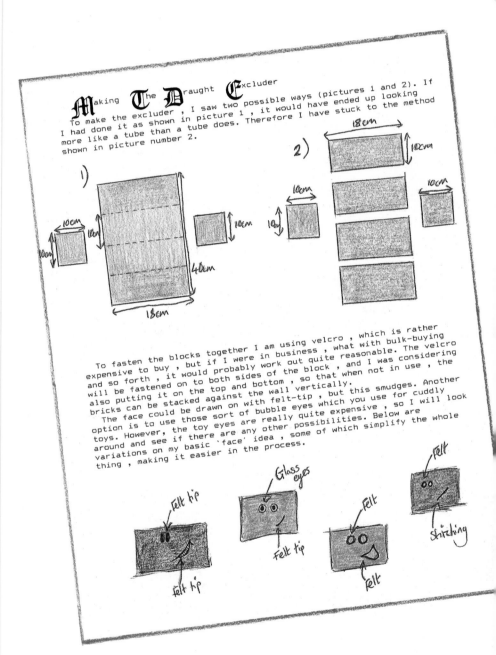

Making The Draught Excluder

To make the excluder, I saw two possible ways (pictures 1 and 2). If I had done it as shown in picture 1, it would have ended up looking more like a tube than a tube does. Therefore I have stuck to the method shown in picture number 2.

To fasten the blocks together I am using velcro, which is rather expensive to buy, but if I were in business, what with bulk-buying and so forth, it would probably work out quite reasonable. The velcro will be fastened on to both sides of the block, and I was considering also putting it on the top and bottom, so that when not in use, the bricks can be stacked against the wall vertically.

The face could be drawn on with felt-tip, but this smudges. Another option is to use those sort of bubble eyes which you use for cuddly toys. However, the toy eyes are really quite expensive, so I will look around and see if there are any other possibilities. Below are variations on my basic 'face' idea, some of which simplify the whole thing, making it easier in the process.

...ow to produce better quality pieces of work, and how to ...satisfactorily.
...almost everything well, although I could have done ...research and go into greater detail on ideas which I ...op.

Evaluation

The one sample brick which I did make was very easy really , and presented no particular problems which I hadn't thought of before-hand. I found some stuffing which worked very well for what I needed it for , it was white and fluffy , and when compressed became very firm and insulatory.

To decide which of the possible methods I should use for creating eyes , I took a blank sheet of the white brushed cotton , and tested each of the methods on it. I found the results rather surprising. Permanant black marker did not , as I thought it would , smudge , but instead came out bold and strong , and was easy to work with. The glass eyes also worked well , although they didn't have the same characterisation to them which was achieved with the marker. On a practical note , I think that they would not have been worth the trouble , possibly causing chipped paintwork and floors , and they could have shattered or been picked of by a small child. (On a safety note , incidentally , I apprieciate that the materials I have used would have had to have been fire-proof if I had been comercially producing this item). The felt eyes were difficult to sew , and looked scruffy and character-less on each of three attempts. I therfore concluded that my best bet was to use a marker pen.

Conclusion

To conclude , I think I can say that I have gone pretty much by other peoples' opinions , and by the results of what I believed to be perfectly fair tests , rather than allowing personal predjudices and pre-conceived ideas to take over. The one exeption to this was in using white as a colour on the excluder; I considered this to be an important part of the product in that a set of plain blocks would probably not go down so well as if there were faces on them. I think this is about the same as the difference between having a multi-coloured 'thing' type draught excluder or a caterpillar style one.

One item which I would have liked to include , but was not able to , was pricing the product. The reason for this was that people only seem to sell poly-cotton , brushed cotton and velcro in far larger quantities than I required.

I also showed the product to the elderly folk who had chosen it from my design list , and some of them asked if I would like to make the rest of the set for them.

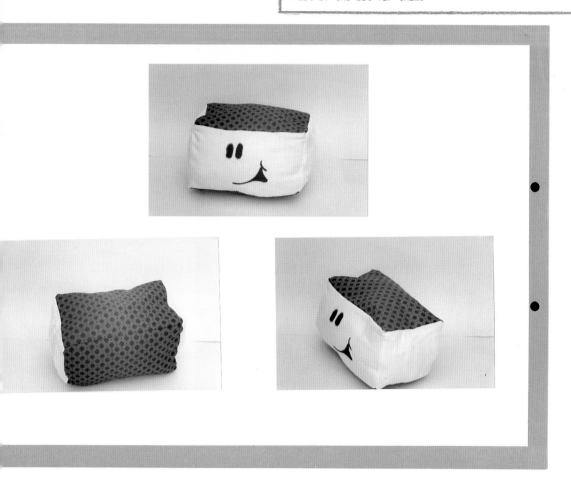

WORKING WITH TEXTILES

LEVEL 6
THEME: KEEPING WARM
CONTEXT: HOME
PROJECT: THERMAL CURTAINS
PUPIL: HANA

Getting started

Aim

To encourage pupils to develop effective investigative techniques by applying them to a specific situation. Pupils were also given an opportunity to understand the difference between subjective and objective value judgements. As pupils were familiar with making subjective judgements they were encouraged to build in tests and investigations to develop their objective evaluation skills. Pupils were limited to the resources of a textiles working environment.

Assessment 1

There is not sufficient recorded evidence to be entirely happy with crediting Te1.6a, but you can infer that Hana must have done considerable research to draw up her list of considerations.
(Evidence for Tes 1.6a, 2.5e.)

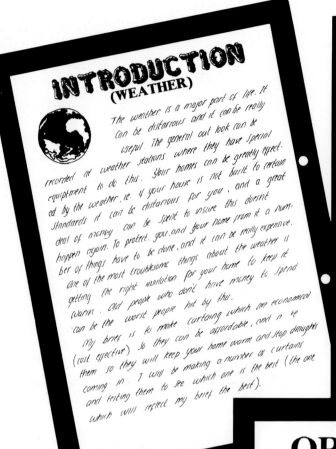

INTRODUCTION (WEATHER)

The weather is a major part of life. It can be disastrous and it can be really useful. The general out look can be recorded at weather stations where they have special equipment to do this. Your homes can be greatly effected by the weather. ie. if your house is not built to certain standards it can be disastrous for you, and a great deal of money can be spent to insure this doesn't happen again. To protect you, and your home from it a number of things have to be done, and it can be really expensive. One of the most troublesome things about the weather is getting the right insulation for your home to keep it warm. Old people who don't have money to spend can be the worst people hit by this.

My brief is to make curtaining which are economical (cost effective) So they can be affordable, and in the them so they will keep your home warm and stop draughts coming in. I will be making a number of curtains and testing them to see which one is the best (the one which will reflect my brief the best).

HYPOTH[...]

Each year there is [...] people who die from [...] conditions. The aim [...] of hypothermia, descr[...] assess the incidence [...] elderly people. Als[...] details of booklets [...]

Definition

Hypothermia is define[...] temperature and is ge[...] temperature drops to [...] an arbitrary cut-off [...] the effects of low bod[...] effect from such cold[...] before that level is [...] of thumb measure.

Symptoms and Treatmen[...]

The outward signs of [...] speech, unsteady move[...] and skin which is cold [...] treatment is a slow r[...] This would usually ent[...] in bed although it is [...] Warm nourishing drink[...] should not be given. [...] circumstances.

The Extent of the Pro[...]

The hypothermic condi[...] undiagnosed as a main [...] elderly people. One [...] standard clinical the[...] 35 deg C and so tempe[...] unrecognised. The nat[...] sufferer is unaware t[...] cold state.

ORDER O[...] WORK[...]

1. Design experiment.

2. Do research into suitability of [...]
   Type and thickness of fabr[...]
   Colour of fabric
   Popularity
   Fibre Contents

3. Choose and cut out fabrics [...]
   linings

4. Make curtains and linings

5. Carry out experiment to f[...]
   Suitable curtain to prevent[...]

HE FACTS

numbers of elderly
e at risk from cold
o define the condition
ognised and treated and
cold conditions among
of further reading and
e.

ow inner body
t when the inner body
This is to some extent
react differently to
e may suffer little ill
thers may be in danger
ever, an accepted rule

drowsiness, slurred
face, mental confusion
most suitable immediate
ent and of the room.
ing well wrapped-up and
of heavy blankets.
recovery but alcohol
called in all

l frequently goes
tor in many deaths of
this is that the
rd temperatures below
evel can go
can also mean that the
ng into a dangerously

IDEAS FOR PROBLEMS

How to keep a young mother healthy and warm in cold weather who is on a set/limited budget

How to keep an elderly person healthy and warm in cold weather who is on a limited budget.

How an elderly person would cope with the changing seasons on a limited budget.

To dress a young child with suitable clothing for the changing seasons of the year on a limited budget.

To dress a growing teenager with suitable clothing for the changing seasons of the year on a limited budget.

To insulate your home from draughts etc in the winter.

How to keep your house warm for winter when there is only 1 or 2 people staying there.

Find out what food is healthy and cheap in winter.

How to stay cool in the summer on a limited or set budget.

MY BRIEF...
TO DESIGN ECONOMICAL CURTAINS WHICH MINIMISE HEAT LOSS AND PREVENT DRAUGHTS COMING INTO YOUR HOME.

WORKING WITH TEXTILES

LEVEL 6
THEME: KEEPING WARM
CONTEXT: HOME
PROJECT: THERMAL CURTAINS
PUPIL: HANA

Developing ideas

Teacher's comments

Hana is an extremely methodical pupil who approached the design and setting up of an experiment to evaluate the effectiveness of two types of curtains, with care and attention to detail. She had no difficulty in understanding the concept of objective evaluation, but in her project notes there are no explicit references to this or to subjective evaluation. Her project suffered from being mainly theoretical as the curtains she made were a suitable size for the experiment and not full size. Even though this was valid in the circumstances, the project could have been extended so that Hana was making curtains for a real person's needs (aesthetic, insulation and cost effective).

Assessment 2

Hana systematically tested her fabrics using standard burn and wash tests. She did this as a safety check having identified the type and colour of fabric in advance. (Ideally this could have been used as a means of justifying the choice of materials.) She researched the process of making curtains before starting work to avoid unforeseen difficulties.
(Evidence for Tes 1.5, 2.5b, 2.5e, 2.6a, 2.6c, 3.6d.)

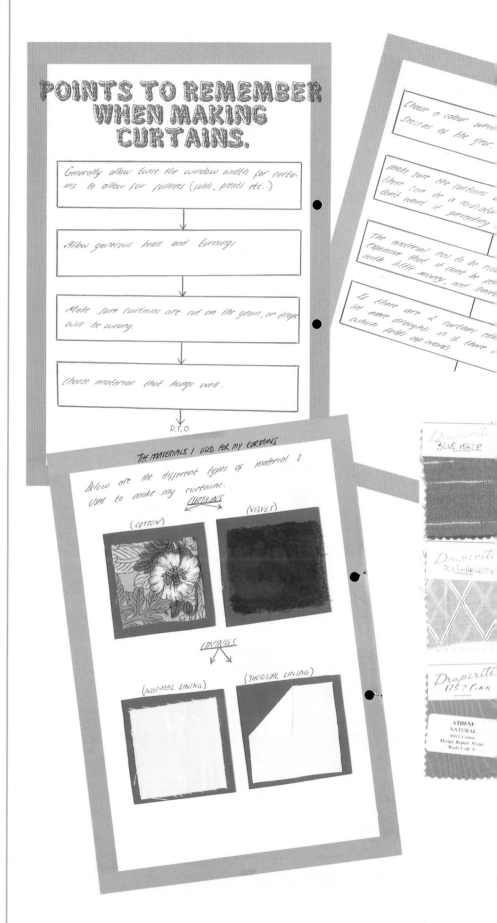

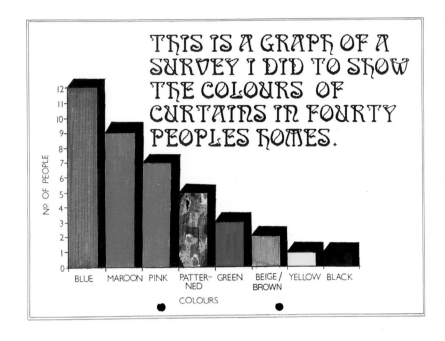

THIS IS A GRAPH OF A SURVEY I DID TO SHOW THE COLOURS OF CURTAINS IN FOURTY PEOPLES HOMES.

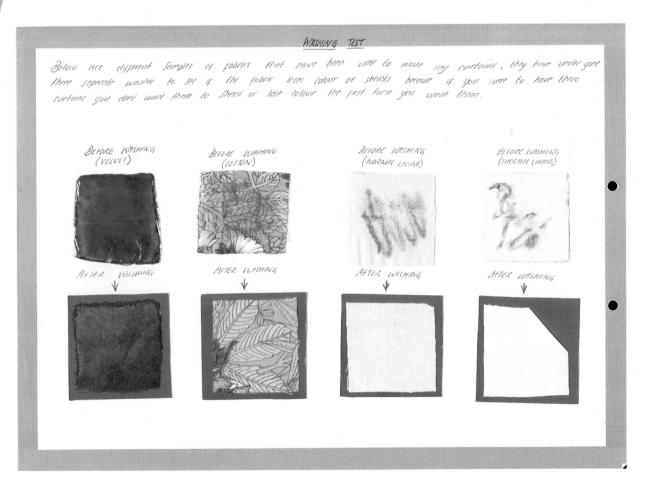

WASHING TEST

Below are different samples of fabrics that have been used to make my curtains, they have under gone three seperate washes to see if the fabric loses colour or shrinks because if you were to have these curtains you dont want them to shrink or lose colour the first time you wash them.

BEFORE WASHING (VELVET)

BEFORE WASHING (COTTON)

BEFORE WASHING (NORMAL LINING)

BEFORE WASHING (THERMAL LINING)

AFTER WASHING

AFTER WASHING

AFTER WASHING

AFTER WASHING

WORKING WITH TEXTILES

LEVEL 6
THEME: KEEPING WARM
CONTEXT: HOME
PROJECT: THERMAL CURTAINS
PUPIL: HANA

Making things happen

Project review

How and when would you have intervened to ensure that Hana recorded all her thinking and decision making?

How would you have structured the project and guided pupils' work, so that pupils were able to tackle a wider range of real issues, so making their working, outcomes and evaluations more concrete?

What other ways can you think of for teaching pupils about value judgements?

Can you think of ways Hana could improve her project and work up to level 7?

Assessment 3

Hana has not given a very full evaluation of her working procedures, she was more concerned to set up a fair scientific-type test. There is evidence for continuous evaluation in the decisions taken during the project. The main area relevant to the project is the choice and use of materials which were thoroughly evaluated by the test. The results show that the thicker fabric with a thermal lining fabric did produce the best insulating curtains - which might have been predicted!

(Evidence of Tes 3.6b, 3.6c, 3.6d, 4.6b, 4.6c.)

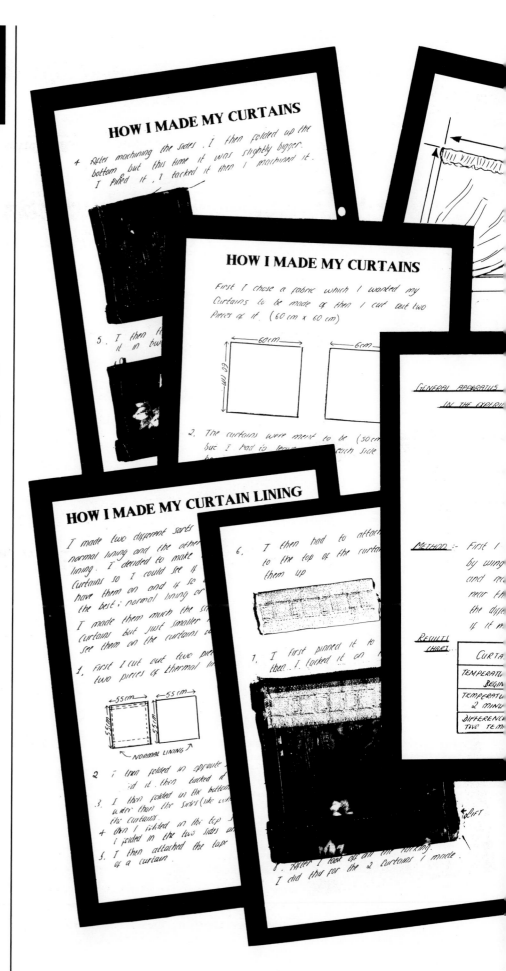

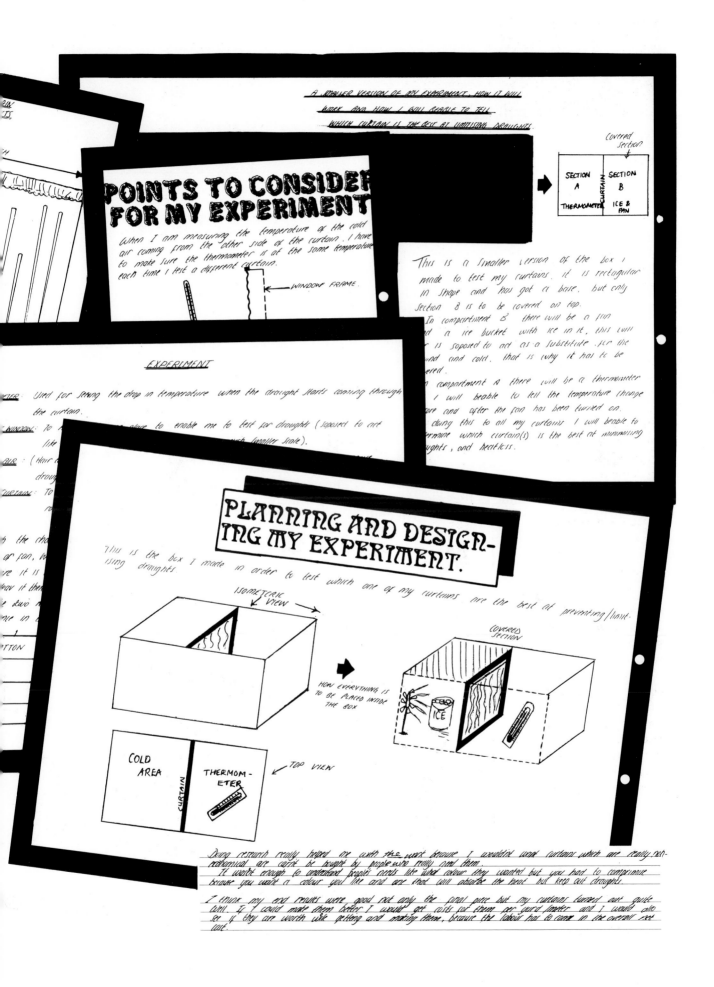

A SMALLER VERSION OF MY EXPERIMENT, HOW IT WILL
WORK AND HOW I WILL BE ABLE TO TELL
WHICH CURTAIN IS THE BEST AT LIMITING DRAUGHTS.

Covered
Section
↓

SECTION A	SECTION B
THERMOMETER	ICE & FAN

(CURTAIN between sections)

POINTS TO CONSIDER FOR MY EXPERIMENT

When I am measuring the temperature of the cold air coming from the other side of the curtain, I have to make sure the thermometer is at the same temperature each time I test a different curtain.

← WINDOW FRAME.

This is a smaller version of the box I made to test my curtains. It is rectangular in shape and has got a base, but only Section B is to be covered on top.
In compartment B there will be a fan and a ice bucket with ice in it, this will is suposed to act as a substitute for the wind and cold, that is why it has to be covered.
In compartment A there will be a thermometer I will be able to tell the temperature change before and after the fan has been turned on.
doing this to all my curtains I will be able to determine which curtain(s) is the best at minimising draughts, and heatloss.

EXPERIMENT

Used for seeing the drop in temperature when the draught starts coming through the curtain.

To ____ place to enable me to test for draughts (suposed to act like ____ with smaller scale).

PLANNING AND DESIGN-ING MY EXPERIMENT.

This is the box I made in order to test which one of my curtains are the best at preventing/limit-ising draughts.

ISOMETRIC VIEW

HOW EVERYTHING IS TO BE PLACED INSIDE THE BOX

COVERED SECTION

ICE

COLD AREA	THERMOM-ETER

(CURTAIN) ← TOP VIEW

Doing research really helped me with the work because I wouldn't want curtains which are really non-economical are can't be bought by people who really need them.
It wasn't enough to understand people's needs like what colour they wanted but you had to compromise because you want a colour you like and one that will absorbe the heat but keep out draughts.

I think my end results were good not only the final piece but my curtains turned out quite well. If I could make them better I would get costs for them per yard/meter and I would also see if they are worth while getting and making them, because the labour has to come in the overall cost.

5 *Planning Assessments*

If we are to plan an effective curriculum for capability, we all need to be clear about *what* capability is, *why* it is important for pupils to develop it and *how* it is built from purposeful connected activities. Without this understanding, assessment will also be problematic as it relies heavily on interpreting performance, in the context of particular experiences, against quite general criteria.

Using the materials presented in this book systematically to address each of the issues referred to in the check list on page 123 will help further understanding of the role of assessment and how it can be used to plan and develop the curriculum.

The check list covers key issues and guiding principles which underpin purposeful, manageable and appropriate assessment related to what is taught. Teachers of d&t can devise their own in-service programme using this chapter as a flexible resource.

TURNING POLICY INTO PRACTICE

1) Start by considering where you are currently in relation to assessment, and where you want to move to.

2) To help you to do this, you can use the check list to identify those issues which are a priority for you and your colleagues.

3) You can then set yourself short, medium and long term goals whereby these priorities can be targetted.

4) Having identified what you are trying to achieve, you will need to devise and detail your plans for the development towards these goals, including any in-service training required. Such

considerations might include:

– what will be achieved and by when?
– how will this be measured?
– who will be responsible for each aspect of the proposed developments?
– how do your plans fit in with the broader picture of any general school or LEA assessment policy and requirements?

There are two aspects to successful assessment: these are making the actual assessments and managing assessment effectively across a d&t department.

MAKING ASSESSMENTS

Planning assessments has as much to do with planning for teaching and learning to take place, as it has to do with creating assessment opportunities. If the curriculum is not geared towards enabling pupils to work capably with a range of contexts, materials, tools and processes when designing and making, then there is no purpose in assessing them.

Consequently, a good starting point for the development of any assessment policy and practice is to evaluate the learning experience which is being planned for pupils in d&t. Using the projects presented in chapters three and four you can identify the issues surrounding the question of what constitutes an appropriate learning experience for the development of capability. Evaluating these for the appropriateness of what pupils are doing and the ways in which they are working, as well as what they achieved, is a useful precursor to evaluating and developing your own teaching programme. The key is to work from your strengths and to build on the expertise of the teachers in your team in

CHECK LIST

• Do you and your colleagues share a view of what it means to be capable in National Curriculum terms for d&t?

• Is there a coherent teaching programme in place which aims to help pupils become capable?

• How will you get pupils to understand what capability is and then to show you how capable they are?

• What will you use as evidence of capability and how will you interpret it?

• How will you develop a consistent approach to interpreting National Curriculum Statements of Attainment?

• What procedures for assessment will need to be established? For example, how often will assessments be carried out? When in the key stage will this happen?

• When and how often will you assess at profile component (PC) level to gain an overall capability level?

• When and how often will you assess against each Attainment Target to gain a more detailed picture?

• How will a summative teacher assessment be reached and agreed between different teachers contributing to a pupil's d&t experience?

• What types of activity are most appropriate for assessment?

• When and how will assessments be recorded?

• What and how much evidence will be retained for any subsequent quality audit?

• What crosschecks will ensure that assessments are consistently to the same standard across the range of subject specialists (home economics, CDT, textiles, art and design, business education, IT) in a school?

• How will pupils' attainments be shared with them as part of the learning process?

• What will be reported to parents (and how) about their child's attainments in d&t?

putting together a d&t programme which promotes progression in capability.

The 'Planning to Assess Learning' chart on p. iv has been devised to focus your planning for pupils' learning and its assessment. Its purpose is to help you to consider what your learning aims for d&t activity are, how to meet them, and how to relate this to assessment. It highlights an essential feature of planning your assessments, i.e. that it is necessary to be clear about what will be assessed and for what purpose. The answer to this question will help to determine the type of activity which you then run. It is helpful to visualise any d&t activity as a vehicle for particular learning aims, as these will determine the type of activity which is appropriate.

For instance, if you are attempting to assess pupils' whole capability, then the activity will need to be organized to allow pupils to demonstrate whole capability (across all ATs) *on that occasion*. Assessing separate aspects of capability by, for example, focusing on the assessment of one Attainment Target at a time, on separate occasions, in different projects and then aggregating these scores, is not a reliable way of judging whole capability. It does nothing more than indicate how pupils separately manage with the processes of each Attainment Target, rather than indicate how capable they are.

However, in some activities you could focus on particular aspects of the ATs more sharply than others for diagnostic assessment purposes, without compromising the development of pupils' holistic capability. This type of assessment will provide clear details of the aspects which you chose to focus on, but will not provide the fuller overview of the capability level at which pupils are operating. It is, however, useful assessment in its own right if you want to sharpen the focus of particular detail for assessment. It is of course possible to chart a developing view of capability through formative assessment – this is quite different from assessing parts of capability and then piecing them together as if they could be aggregated into a meaningful whole. Being clear about the purpose of any assessment, and where it fits within a programme of learning, is crucial.

For instance, on each occasion where assessments are being made, you could ask whether the purpose is:

• to diagnose strengths and weaknesses with a view to helping pupils to progress,

- to build a formative picture of attainment and monitor pupils' progress,
- to make a summative judgement of pupils' capability at a particular point in time.

The crucial point is to be clear about what you are attempting to assess on any particular occasion, so that the most appropriate type of activity can be chosen as a vehicle for that assessment, and so that the resulting assessment information is not taken out of context – seen for something that it isn't.

MANAGING ASSESSMENTS

A positive step for any team is to negotiate, and renegotiate, a shared understanding of what it means to be teaching pupils to be capable. Then to identify what constitutes an appropriate key stage programme of learning through which your pupils will acquire and develop capability. On the basis of these shared understandings and principles it then becomes possible to plan, as a team, a coherent curriculum experience for pupils which ensures learning and progression. This programme of learning should be based upon the Programme of Study for d&t, and planned and structured to ensure that, over the key stage, pupils acquire and develop the selected knowledge, skills and understanding that they need to become capable in d&t terms, and to operate as design technologists.

You will then need to turn your attention to how assessment, for key stage 3 d&t, is currently conducted in your school. For instance, is each member of the d&t team assessing pupils' capability against National Curriculum criteria, or is each subject area within d&t assessing to its own particular criteria perhaps disconnected from National Curriculum? If the latter is the case, you will need to consider how you are going to move to a position where individual d&t teachers are making their assessments against National Curriculum criteria, otherwise their efforts may result in qualities and abilities other than d&t capability being assessed. Aggregating and reconciling these separate and disparate pieces of assessment data, across the d&t department, into a capability view will be unmanageable.

There are a number of strategies which can be adopted in response to this challenge, and to ensure a mananageable system for making assessments.

Assessment needs to be planned and carried

out as a team. This does not mean that individual teachers are not responsible for making their own assessments of pupils. Nor should it imply that there needs to be some vastly elaborate system for administering assessment. Rather it means that there must be a shared view within the department of what is being assessed and how it will be practically managed. You may consider it advisable that someone on the team is responsible for co-ordinating assessment across the d&t department, or for a particular year group. This might be a role which is shared or rotated year by year.

Consistent interpretations of the SoA will be aided by teachers working together to discuss how and why they are making their various judgements of pupils' capability. To this end running 'agreement' trials with your colleagues is a beneficial way of ensuring that such a common understanding develops. The projects presented in this book provide a useful resource bank which can be suitably employed for this purpose. They will spark debate about how we judge pupils' capability, as well as how we interpret the evidence from d&t activity.

The key to managing assessment, as well as to making valid and reliable assessments, is to clarify what it means for pupils to be capable; to develop a teaching model where teachers use their experience and expertise to enable pupils to become capable; to develop ways of assessing their developing capability.

We need to focus on ways of doing this not just in terms of satisfying the statutory requirements, but to our own satisfaction as professionals involved in teaching and learning.